CHURCHES, SECTS AND RELIGIOUS PARTIES

CHURCHES, SECTS AND RELIGIOUS PARTIES

BY

G. W. BUTTERWORTH, Litt.D.

LONDON
SOCIETY FOR PROMOTING
CHRISTIAN KNOWLEDGE
NORTHUMBERLAND AVENUE, W.C. 2

First published, 1936

MADE IN GREAT BRITAIN

CONTENTS

PART I

THE HISTORIC CHURCHES

CHAPTER   PAGE

   I. The Church of England - - - - 9

  II. Catholicism - - - - - - 13

 III. Protestantism - - - - - 17

 IV. Anglo-Catholicism - - - - - 21

   V. Evangelicalism - - - - - 26

 VI. Liberal Evangelicalism - - - 31

 VII. Modernism - - - - - - 36

VIII. The Roman Catholic Church - - - 42

 IX. The Eastern Orthodox Church - - - 55

PART II

THE FREE CHURCHES

   I. Congregationalists - - - - - 73

  II. Presbyterians - - - - - - 78

 III. Baptists - - - - - - - 83

 IV. Quakers - - - - - - - 88

   V. Unitarians - - - - - - 93

 VI. Methodists - - - - - - 98

 VII. The " Catholic Apostolic " Church - - 103

VIII. The Salvation Army - - - - 108

PART III

VARIOUS SECTS AND DOCTRINES

CHAPTER   PAGE

I. BRITISH-ISRAELISM - - - - - 115

II. "GREAT PYRAMID FUNDAMENTALS" - - - 119

III. CHRISTIAN SCIENCE - - - - - 123

IV. SPIRITUALISM - - - - - - 128

V. CHRISTADELPHIANISM - - - - - 133

VI. JUDGE RUTHERFORD - - - - - 137

VII. THEOSOPHY - - - - - - 141

VIII. ROSICRUCIANISM - - - - - - 147

PART I

THE HISTORIC CHURCHES

NEARLY all the chapters of this book have appeared in the *Southwark Diocesan Gazette*. I make no apology for the fact that they are written from the standpoint of the Church of England, my spiritual mother, whom I love and am proud to serve. Nevertheless, I have tried to be accurate and fair in describing other bodies; and I recognise that we shall not experience the full glory of Christian life and doctrine until all who worship God in Christ have brought their contribution to the Catholic Church that one day shall be.

G. W. BUTTERWORTH.

CHAPTER I

THE CHURCH OF ENGLAND

THE Church of England claims to be the historic Church of this country, with a continuous existence going back to Roman-British times. The claim is made not with studied publicity, which we should regard as needless. Rather it is assumed, as naturally as a grown man assumes his identity with himself when a boy. The Prayer Book is based upon this assumption; and every cathedral and almost every old parish church reveal it by the care with which the records of the past are cherished. Lists of rectors show no break except during the short Commonwealth period, when the Church came near to being replaced by an entirely different system.

At some time towards the end of the second century missionaries, probably from Gaul, planted the beginnings of Christianity here. When, after the Edict of Milan, the Church in the West was freed from persecution and could pursue its life in peace, a Council was held at Arles in Gaul, in A.D. 314, at which three bishops from Britain were present. This British Church was driven into Wales and Cornwall during the Saxon invasions of the fifth and sixth centuries. But a fresh beginning was made when Augustine was sent by Gregory the Great, Bishop of Rome, in A.D. 597, to evangelise this country. From this new effort, with the aid of Celtic missionaries from Scotland, the Church in England was built up again.

Englishmen owe an immense debt of gratitude to Gregory and Augustine. The story of Gregory's noble plan, and Augustine's efforts to accomplish it, as told by Bede in his *Church History of the English Nation*, is immortal. But this gives Rome no right to claim perpetual supremacy over the Church of England, any more than we ought to claim supremacy over the many Churches founded by the labours of Englishmen in remote parts of the earth.

When Augustine came, and for nearly three centuries after, Britain was not a united country, but a collection of States hostile to each other and continually at war. Yet in the seventh century Theodore visited the Church in all parts of the country, held synods of clergy, fixed the boundaries of dioceses, and established himself as " Archbishop of the English People." Thus the Church attained a corporate, united life centuries before the State.

At the Norman Conquest the Saxons became a conquered people, and many Saxon bishops gave place to Normans. But the Church as a whole went on its way almost unaltered. There followed several centuries of glorious work, the building of majestic cathedrals everywhere, and the foundation of monasteries whose ruins give us but a faint idea of the genius and devotion of their originators. The great names of this period, such as Lanfranc, Anselm, Langton, Becket, Grossetete, and William of Wykeham, form a company of whom any nation might be proud; and though they were human and not free from faults, their lives are untarnished by any vulgar ambition for worldly power, such as too often characterised the feudal ecclesiastics of the Continent and even the pontiffs of Rome itself.

In this period Rome was the recognised centre of Christendom in the West. In the East men looked to Constantinople. But the Roman bishops were not content with a primacy of honour. They wished to control the Church, by nominating their own men to its livings and dignities, and by exacting vast sums of money to pay for the expenses of the Roman court. History gives ample record of the protests made by England against such conduct. The *Statute of Provisors* in 1351 forbade Papal appointments to English benefices, and the *Statute of Præmunire* in 1353 forbade Englishmen to carry appeals abroad, by which it was well known that Rome was meant. So great was the power of the Popes that these statutes were not successful in abolishing the evils they aimed at; but the fact that both were re-enacted later on shows the strength and persistence of English feeling.

Hitherto the quarrels of England and Rome concerned government, not doctrine. But in the fourteenth century we hear from John Wiclif and his Lollard followers the beginnings of discontent with Roman doctrine, not the age-long doctrine of the Catholic Church, but new interpretations of it and new practices. The Roman Church, too, was corrupt, and abuses which were patent to all men, and which the Church apparently could not reform, caused misgivings in many hearts. The monastic system also had passed its first glory, and in the fifteenth century pious benefactors founded colleges and schools rather than monasteries. So we come to the breach with Rome under Henry VIII. Though the occasion of that event was unfortunate, it is clear that England was glad to be free from Papal domination. Henry's notion of a Catholic Church independent of Rome expressed the desires of the mass of Englishmen.

When once a revolution begins, its end cannot be foreseen. And the Reformation was a revolution. In every other country where it was accepted either the ancient ministry, or the creeds, or the traditional forms of worship, or all of them, were ruthlessly sacrificed. In England alone was the necessary purification and simplification effected without the loss of anything essential. This was done of set purpose, and not by accident. Looking back, there are few who do not wish that some things had been ordered otherwise. But considering the difficulties it is a miracle that the Church of England should have preserved so unmistakably her Catholic character.

In doing this she lost first the Separatists and then the Presbyterians. Whether these further breaches in the unity of the Church were avoidable or no, who can tell? The Church of England had chosen a middle path, between Rome and Dissent, and to that she resolutely held. The loss of the Methodists is perhaps of another order, due to want of enthusiasm within the Church. Yet here, too, it is easier to judge after the event than to act rightly at the critical moment.

During the last century and a half the Church of England has expanded into the Anglican Communion, a vast association of federated Churches spread throughout the whole world. More than that, she has produced a constant succession of students and thinkers whose labours have enriched the whole Church. In no Communion is thought more free than in the Church of England. That is why we have differences. We talk more of these differences than of our underlying unity; nevertheless, we form one Church, and not an agglomeration of parties. The chapters which follow deal with several aspects of the Church, yet many of her members hesitate to call themselves either Evangelical or Anglo-Catholic or Modernist; for they try to hold the essence of all three, which is by no means impossible.

CHAPTER II

CATHOLICISM

THE word " catholic " is a Greek word meaning " universal." It came into use when heretical bodies arose in the second century. These were personal, local and partial in character, and a term was needed to define the historic Church as contrasted with them. " It needs no long discourse to prove," says Clement of Alexandria, writing about 200 A.D., " that the merely human assemblies which they have instituted were later in time than the Catholic Church." Clement goes on to say that " unity is a characteristic of the true, the really ancient Church," which the leaders of heresies " strive to break up into many sects."

Thus the term came to distinguish the ancient society, with its organised life, going back to the Apostles and to our Lord Himself. To this society the preaching of the gospel had been entrusted. Consequently, the chief idea conveyed by Catholicism is that of the corporate nature of our religion. Christianity is not a teaching flung out into the air, so to speak, for every one to catch as he can. It is a historic movement, rooted in a visible society. And this society, in the succession of its bishops, contains within itself the means for its own continuance. It is an organised army, fighting God's battle against evil. It is also an ark, as we say in the Baptismal service, sheltering human souls as they pass through the waves of this troublesome world.

Nowadays many strong Protestants value the corporate nature of Christianity. But as a rule Protestantism has overstressed the individual side, making religion little more than a means of personal salvation. Here it contrasts with Catholicism. Most people, and especially the young, feel an inspiration in belonging to a body, in which they can work for God here and now, which they could never feel in seeking for themselves escape from hell or entrance into heaven.

There is a widespread feeling to-day, extending beyond the bounds of the Church, that the Catholic ministry, in spite of defects and mistakes of human origin, has been a safeguard for religion. If from the beginning men had been left without such guidance, to choose entirely for themselves, and to split up into sects and parties at the whim of every self-styled leader, what would Christianity have come to? The steadying influence of the great Church must have counted for much. But this thought brings us to the question of Authority. Catholicism has always stressed Authority, whereas Protestantism has exalted Private Judgment. How do we learn about divine things? Is it by being taught them by such as have authority? Or are we our own authorities, each groping about to seek whatever truth we may be fortunate enough to find? Clearly, in practical life, everyone uses both methods. To speak of " the religions of authority and the religion of the Spirit " (the title of a book by M. Sabatier), as if a system like Catholicism, in which Authority plays its part, was necessarily opposed to the inspiration of the Spirit, is not justifiable.

The fact is that Authority is just as necessary in religion as it is in physics or astronomy. As science holds an accumulated fund of knowledge, and passes it on from student to student, so the Church has an accumulated experience of God's dealings with man, which she passes on to her children. A religious man can no more begin at the beginning than can a scientist. We teach our children what we believe to be true, and they must build on that basis. So the Church teaches us all. And the venerable forms in which Church teaching has been enshrined, such as the Creeds, are entitled to respect, even if a man does not see his way clearly through them at first.

Truths learned from Authority must be made our own through experience. Authority becomes harmful only when it forbids us to use our own experience, stifling free thought and discussion; or when it tries to mould the plastic minds of children into a set pattern. This is happening in many countries to-day in the political sphere, and it is one of the most serious signs of our times. No one who is acquainted with history can deny that Church authority has been abused in the past, and is being abused to-day. But it was not so in the beginning. In the New Testament we find a vivid, powerful and definite faith; yet what a wonderful freedom pervades it all! And Catholicism, which has its roots in the New Testament, need not be a rigid and repressive system. While truth cannot alter, our modes of apprehending and expressing it are likely to change as knowledge deepens. The Church must allow for that. That there can be a free Catholic atmosphere in a world-wide Church is proved by the very existence of the Anglican Communion, whose members may indeed thank God that He has " set their feet in a large room." Only those who are secretly afraid that their faith is not true need resort to coercion in order to defend it.

But of all things peculiar to Catholicism, worship is the most distinctive. Every body of Christians which has separated from the old Church has at once completely changed the forms and atmosphere of Catholic worship. Luther, it is true, would have kept to the ancient ways if he could, but events were too strong for him. If a visitor from another planet were to inspect, let us say, St. Paul's and the Roman Catholic Cathedral at Westminster, or Westminster Abbey, he would at once conclude that all these were buildings used for the same purpose. No differences of architecture or varieties of adornment could obscure that fact. If he went on to a tiny village church he would place that in the same category, the difference being analogous to that between a manor house and a cottage. But if he continued his travels, and inspected the City Temple and other Nonconformist churches, and had nothing but the inner arrangement of the buildings to go by, he would have no reason to connect them with the first ones he had seen. For in the first the central feature was an altar, placed where all could see it as they entered the building, while other accessories, such as pulpit, reading and prayer desks, were tucked away at the sides. In the second the pulpit was given pre-eminence. The place was made for preaching; and if it had other uses they were not clear.

When our visitor began to ask questions, we should explain to him, in simple language, that the altar was the holy place where God met His children, where they worshipped Him and were fed by Him with heavenly food; that we approached God not, as it were, in the void, but through certain outward signs which He had appointed; and that this was the purpose for which the churches were built. All else was subsidiary, and could, indeed, be dispensed with if necessary; the altar was essential. For a man does not begin to be a " Catholic " because he puts on certain vestments or burns incense; he is one when he worships God in the ancient sacramental way which Jesus Christ Himself instituted, and which has been the heart of Catholic worship ever since.

Sacramental worship implies that material things are not unspiritual, but can be made vehicles of grace and truth. Consequently, Catholicism has always cherished art in its various forms —painting, sculpture, architecture. Protestantism, on the contrary, has generally feared and suspected art in religion. The glorious Gothic cathedrals, which everyone admires, were built for sacramental worship. That is the soul which produced their grandeur and beauty. And if such worship should ever fail they would remain like bodies with the life departed, fantastic figures, more pathetic even than the Pyramids.

CHAPTER III

PROTESTANTISM

IF the ordinary Englishman is certain of one thing, it is that he is a Protestant. The title is now part of our history, taught to children in every school and sworn to by our Kings when they are crowned. But what exactly does it mean?

Here the Englishman has a ready answer. It means that he protests against the Church of Rome. This opposition, though generally subconscious, may become articulate at any moment if something occurs to awaken it. All who deal with Englishmen must take it into account. And it has a clear and intelligible origin. It dates from the reign of Mary, a queen who, embittered by her mother's sufferings and her own disappointed life, sought to restore England to the Roman obedience by the fires of Smithfield.

It is probable that no one has ever done more harm to Christian unity than this queen, in the few years of her unhappy reign. Every English child, reading her history at his most impressionable age, feels a revulsion which he can never overcome. Other persecutors have been more cruel than Mary, or have had greater numbers of victims, but her persecution was foolish as much as it was wrong. It wholly misunderstood the needs of the time and the temper of Englishmen.

But resentment, however justifiable, at deeds performed four hundred years ago cannot provide a sure foundation for religious faith. Perhaps the reason why so many Englishmen, nominally members of the Church of England, are hopelessly vague about their religion is to be found in this fact. They ask themselves, " What do I protest against?" instead of, " What do I stand for?" Religion must be a positive, not a negative, thing.

And, curiously enough, the term Protestantism, though in common acceptation it is now definitely negative, was not originally so. When Luther's reforming movement spread in Germany, struggles took place to decide which should be supreme, the old Church or the Lutheran bodies. At Speyer in 1526 it was decided by the assembled princes that the religion adopted by the ruler should be the religion of his subjects. Under this compromise Lutherans were assured of safety if they lived under a Lutheran prince. But in 1529, at a subsequent Diet at Speyer, this arrangement was cancelled and Lutheran princes and people alike were bidden to return to the old ways. On this a number of Lutheran princes drew up their famous " Protestation," declaring that they would not surrender their liberty of framing a religious system for their dominions in accordance with their conscience. So they were called Protestants, and, although Luther disliked the title, it gradually spread to all his followers. Zwinglians and Calvinists, however, were for long at enmity with Lutherans, and it was only much later that the name Protestant was widened to include them.

When the Prayer Book was first framed, Protestantism was not a sufficiently important term to be even considered for mention. Nor was there need to mention it; for it is clear that the compilers of the Prayer Book desired to keep more closely in touch with the ancient ways than the Lutherans did. But the term has never found a place either in succeeding editions of the Prayer Book or in the Canons. In the seventeenth century, however, it was frequently used to describe the Church of England, in opposition both to Romanists and Puritans. Charles I. declared his attachment to the Protestant religion, thereby disavowing both Popery and Puritanism. It is in this sense that the word appears in the coronation oath; the King must be a member of the Church of England. But in later times those who dissented from the Church of England began to be called " Protestant dissenters "; and thus the term Protestant acquired its present wide connotation, describing anyone who stands outside the Church of Rome.

A movement such as Protestantism, which combines within

itself so many divergent teachings and tendencies, is hard to describe. Luther stood for " Justification by Faith " and by faith only. But Luther was a man who had passed through a deep spiritual experience. Catholic theology has never denied that justification comes by faith, but it adds the very necessary qualification that faith must be made evident through works. To that most men would now agree.

Then there is the question of authority. Protestants looked to the Bible as the one and only source of their doctrine, ignoring the history of the Church. There were great gains in thus turning men's attention to the sacred writings and stimulating individual religion. But there were losses, too, for Protestants claimed the right to interpret the Bible as each thought fit, which resulted in a multitude of sects and opinions. And modern knowledge of the Bible has made the Protestant position extremely difficult.

Dr. Inge, in his volume entitled *Protestantism*, in Benn's Six-penny Library, says that " the spirit of Protestantism, when it understands itself, holds that there is no infallible authority any-where, but that men are educated by what Dean Church called the gifts of civilisation, and by the Holy Spirit, whose operations are now often called religious experience." The weakness of Dr. Inge's argument is that, in dealing with Catholicism, he treats all its ugly history as essential to the system, while the many equally undesirable features of Protestantism are passed over as accidental. Both Protestantism and Catholicism have been guilty of persecution, tyranny and obscurantism; and if these evils are products of the system in the one case they are equally so in the other.

It would be more true to say that Protestantism, taken generally, represents an awakening of the human spirit to its true freedom and worth, and rebellion against any authority that would cramp and enslave that spirit. So far as it is that it may certainly claim our sympathy, for in such an awakening we feel a breath of fresh air coming from the pages of the New Testament itself. In England we have a passion for liberty, which I hope we may never lose; but any observer can see that in the history of Protestantism liberty has often run mad. Group has seceded from group for trivial reasons. In the first thrills of their newly found freedom, in the sixteenth century, Protestants flung away the creeds, the ancient ministry, ordered liturgical worship, and many other things, which some of them are now painfully trying to recover. And although some breach in the unity of Western Christendom was probably inevitable owing to the harsh attitude of Rome, the multiplication of sects was undoubtedly an evil.

Englishmen as a rule are restrained in their revolutions. And just as in political life we have managed, as yet, to combine freedom with order, so in the Church of England we have a genuine and, I believe, a successful attempt to combine the essence of Protestantism with the order and beauty of the Catholic tradition.

CHAPTER IV

ANGLO-CATHOLICISM

It is the mark of a living body that it can act in different ways to meet different circumstances, preserving its identity through change. Judged by this test the Church of England may claim to be alive. For in spite of Acts of Uniformity she is not, and never has been, uniform. If she were she would be a machine, not a body. And the succession of movements within the Church, each arising to remedy defects in its predecessor, bears witness to the presence of God among us. Evangelicals stressed personal piety rightly and well. Then came others to exalt the Church, the divine society, with its rites and sacraments, things which Evangelicals had held too lightly. The Church needs both. If one or other is missing, she is like a man with one lung—existing indeed, but incapable of the strenuous activities of life.

About a hundred years ago a few men in Oxford felt that the Church was in danger. There were ideas abroad, summed up in the term " liberalism," which they disliked and feared. Now true liberalism is a noble thing. But it may be misused to mean simply shallowness. In religion a man may call himself liberal because he believes that one creed is as good as another, that everything in Christianity which appears divine or mysterious should be abandoned and the Church made nothing more than the mouthpiece of general opinion. Because the Church of England had been honourably associated with the State for many centuries, politicians supposed that she did not count as a source of independent authority. The Oxford Movement was a protest against this.

Certainly the Church herself, through her slackness, was largely to blame for the poor repute in which she was held. Nor was the

State wholly unreasonable. Great efforts were being made, by the Reform Bill, the Corn Laws and Roman Catholic Emancipation, to provide a humaner life for the masses of our people. Bishops, on the other hand, showed a persistent tendency to do the wrong thing; they actually voted against the Reform Bill.

The Church was badly led; she was unconscious of her character, her dignity and responsibilities. The Oxford men, Keble, Pusey and the rest, loved the Church with a deep affection. They loved the Prayer Book, the old book of 1662 which scarcely anyone to-day finds sufficient. They took it seriously, believing that when it appointed services it meant them to be held; when fast days, it meant them to be observed. When it ordered the recitation of the Creeds, and spoke of the Catholic Church, it meant to indicate that the Church of England was part of the ancient, continuous, visible society which reached back to apostolic days. Bishops were Catholic bishops, not feudal lords or State officials. They were to be treated with deep respect and to be obeyed, so long as it was remembered that they were bound by the Church's law equally with clergy and laity. Rome was part of the Catholic Church, but she had been guilty of many errors, having distorted some parts of the primitive faith and made unwarranted additions to it.

The leaders of the Oxford Movement were as vigorous as Wesley, but their medium was the printed word rather than emotional sermons, and they appealed to the intelligent section of the Church, in particular to the clergy, through the *Tracts for the Times*. It was *Tract No. 90*, written by Newman, which caused the most intense opposition. People thought that the Thirty-Nine Articles were inconsistent with a Catholic view of the Church. Newman maintained that this was not so; the Articles were carefully phrased and could all be understood in a Catholic sense. What they condemned was Romish errors, not true Catholic doctrine. Though a few of Newman's arguments may be strained, his main contention was sound enough, as most competent students would admit to-day. But great excitement was aroused then, and the treatment which Newman received led to his secession to Rome a few years later.

After this the Movement was divided. A small number, altogether despairing of the Church of England, followed Newman to Rome. But the greater part worked on under difficulties, and it is from them that what is called Anglo-Catholicism has developed, although the latter has many differences from the Tractarianism of a century ago. For the whole Church of England is indebted to the Oxford Movement. Increased diligence of bishops and clergy, more reverent administration and reception of the sacraments, and a deeper sense of the divine origin of the Church —all this is largely traceable to the Movement.

But Anglo-Catholicism is its lineal descendant. Anglo-Catholics give a supreme position to the Eucharist, regarding it as the highest act of worship. Music and ceremonial of the utmost dignity and beauty are therefore appropriate to it. To allow for these, communions are made early, and the High Celebration reserved for solemn devotion. Developments in this direction during the nineteenth century, and particularly the introduction of eucharistic vestments, gave rise to much controversy. The ordinary man, finding the new customs strange, and seeing how closely, in outward appearance, they resembled those of the Church of Rome, concluded not unnaturally that the Movement was leading Romewards. In this belief he was supported by the steady stream of converts to Rome from the time of Newman onwards.

It is doubtful, however, whether Anglo-Catholicism has helped Rome much. The times were ripe for a reversion to Catholic ideas and worship, so long dormant in England. Converts to Rome are always well advertised, and their numbers probably exaggerated. Many of the most prominent, too, have come, and still do come, from strongly Evangelical families, passing from one extreme to another by a natural psychological process. The tide of Catholic feeling in the Church of England has probably kept far more people from Rome than it has sent there. Roman controversialists, who are acute observers, concentrate most of their attention on our Church in its Catholic aspect. Bare Protestantism they have little cause to fear.

Whereas Evangelicalism centres round the experiences of the individual soul, Catholicism dwells on the life of the corporate society, the Church. This gives to worship an atmosphere hard to describe but easy to feel. The sense of continuity with the past and communion with the unseen world is fostered by constant remembrance of the saints and by prayers for the departed. The ancient Church hymns, objective, dramatic and permeated by a strong faith in the Incarnation, harmonise with this, particularly when sung to their traditional melodies.

> "The Royal Banners forward go,
> The Cross shines forth in mystic glow
> Where He in Flesh, our flesh Who made,
> Our sentence bore, our ransom paid."

These noble lines reveal an aspect of the Passion which might be forgotten but for Catholic worship. Anglo-Catholics value the monastic life and have striven to revive it, with more success among women than among men, although the three great Communities of men at Cowley, Mirfield and Kelham have rendered valuable service to the Church. They maintain also the doctrine of Apostolic Succession, which means that ministerial grace is transmitted solely through bishops by an unbroken chain going back to the Apostles. Although the Prayer Book does not enunciate this doctrine, our Church practice since the Reformation has tacitly assumed it; for we do not, in fact, allow others than episcopally ordained men to minister in our churches. The succession is reasonably clear from the beginning of the second century; before that full evidence is lacking, and we are reduced to conjecture based upon our opinion of what the will of Christ or the practice of the Apostles is likely to have been.

The Tractarians appealed to the Councils of the undivided Church, before the schism of East and West, as their standard of faith and practice. They rejected all later Roman additions and developments. Anglo-Catholics generally go beyond this and look to the " Western " Church—that is, to Rome—as a guide to living Catholicism. But the varieties of opinion here are many, ranging from the sturdy upholder of " English " customs and strict Prayer Book doctrine to a number who are ready to accept everything Roman, including the Papacy.

In 1859 the English Church Union was founded in order to uphold the Catholic position in the Church of England. After the war the more restless members of the party started a new venture, the Anglo-Catholic Congress, with the object of " converting " England to the Catholic faith. After some years of uneasy strain the two organisations have been brought together in the " Church Union."

The strength of Anglo-Catholicism has been already indicated. Its weaknesses are an inadequate appreciation of the English character, which needs different ways of expressing its religion from those of the peoples of Italy, France or Spain; and also a lack of profound theological thought. The Tractarians possessed a theology, but their successors have discarded that without being able to replace it by a better. Consequently they have too often to fall back upon Rome. Pastors who find a religious technique that, in a limited way, can be said to " work "—Evangelicals with their " conversion," Groupists with their " sharing," and Anglo-Catholics with the Mass, Confession and their accessories—are tempted to suppose that no further thought is necessary. Fortunately there are, among Anglo-Catholics, a number of able men who are boldly facing theological problems. The authors of *Essays Catholic and Critical,* and perhaps still more Knox and Milner-White in their brilliant reply to Father Vernon, *One God and Father of Us All,* have drunk deeply at the Modernist well. Though they are somewhat suspect of the rank and file, it is probably with such men as these that the future of Anglo-Catholicism lies.

CHAPTER V

EVANGELICALISM

WHAT is an Evangelical? One, I suppose, who believes in, or preaches, the Gospel. But that surely includes us all. The Gospel, however, is a large thing, and men grasp it in different ways, according to their special needs and temperaments. Even in the New Testament the message of Christ is presented in one way by St. Paul and in another by, let us say, St. James, whose work Luther, in a rash moment, called an "epistle of straw." Evangelicals are those who stress the personal side of religion, the sense of forgiveness through Christ, and the warm and living communion of the soul with its Redeemer. This kind of religion is by no means confined to Evangelicals; but they gave it a special emphasis in England at a time when the Church as a whole seemed to have forgotten it. This time was the eighteenth century.

The low state of religious life in that century may of course be exaggerated. We know from *The Deserted Village* and other literature that saintly clergy were by no means extinct. You will often find on notice boards in church porches or vestries how benefactors were continually giving money to the Church and its schools. But when all is said, a state of things was allowed then which would horrify us now. The Rev. G. R. Balleine, in his book *A History of the Evangelical Party,* calls that time the "Glacial Epoch" of the Church of England. "Puritan enthusiasm had been driven out at the Restoration, and High Church enthusiasm had departed with the Nonjurors; only the cautious and colourless remained, Laodiceans, whose ideal Church was neither hot nor cold." Hundreds of parishes in the country had but one service a week, and that taken by a curate who galloped from village to village, serving as many as he could on a single day. The incumbents who should have taken these services were non-resident, claiming the income but acknowledging no duty. Communions were very infrequent, even a monthly one being rare in many districts. Bishops did little to interfere, for they were often the worst offenders, holding numbers of appointments as a means of enriching themselves and their families.

Into a state of affairs like this came Wesley and Whitefield, preaching the necessity of individual conversion, and shocking the sedate Church by their " enthusiasm " and unconventional methods. But the Methodists unwittingly created an organisation which they could not control. Against Wesley's wishes it broke away from the Church. There were some, however, who sympathised with Wesley and yet remained within the Church, working in their own parishes. These were the Evangelicals. At first they worked under difficulties, for their teaching was suspect to the authorities, and they were denied preferment. To overcome this they obtained afternoon Lectureships at City churches. These Lectureships, some of which still exist, were independent of the Rectors, and in some cases long struggles took place between them and the new lecturers. At St. Dunstan's, Fleet Street, the church-wardens complained of the large crowds of non-parishioners who assembled on Sunday afternoons to hear the Rev. William Romaine, a pious and learned Evangelical, preach. They impeded Romaine in every possible way, refusing to light or warm the church, so that for several years he preached in the dark, till at last the Bishop interfered.

South London has many interesting connexions with the early Evangelicals. Besides " the seraphic Mr. Jones," junior chaplain of St. Saviour's, Southwark, from 1753-1762, there was Henry Venn, who ministered at Clapham before going to Huddersfield. Around Clapham Parish Church there grew up an association of worthy laymen, rich and influential, who made it their chief aim in life to promote evangelical piety. William Wilberforce, Henry Thornton and Zachary Macaulay were the nucleus of the " Clapham Sect," whose long struggle to free the slaves will never be forgotten. This work, together with the philanthropy of Lord Shaftesbury, is something which Evangelicals have every reason to be proud of; for it shows their religion to have been dynamic and capable of transforming not only individual lives, but the life of the community. Another light of the movement was Selina, Countess of Huntingdon, who invited society to her " spiritual routs," where her preachers endeavoured to convert them. An important layman, the Earl of Dartmouth, joined the movement through these gatherings, and used his money to buy livings for the Evangelical clergy. Lady Huntingdon established chapels wherever she had a house—at Brighton, Tunbridge Wells, Bath and other fashionable resorts; but she was an imperious person, and separated from the Church because the law then in force would not permit her to open a chapel in Clerkenwell. Her chaplains thereupon left her, and she became the founder of " Lady Huntingdon's Connexion," which was staffed by her lay preachers.

Mr. Balleine says that while the Methodists claimed that the world was their parish, the Evangelicals were in danger of making the parish their world. This must not be taken too seriously, for Evangelicals in this period have the credit of founding the Church Missionary Society. But there were certainly among them clergy of remarkable zeal, who applied themselves with the true pastoral spirit to the spiritual welfare of their flocks. Grimshaw of Haworth, for instance, who used to go out in the hymn before the sermon with his riding-whip to gather in any who had forgotten the time of the service! Some people complained of his unconventional ways, but the Archbishop replied : " We cannot find fault with Mr. Grimshaw when he is instrumental in bringing so many to the Lord's Table." Another interesting man was Thomas Jones, Vicar of Creaton, who used to invite the neighbouring clergy every year in the week after Easter to what would now be called a retreat. But the Bishop at last became alarmed at this strange custom, and forbade the use of the church for such a purpose. And there were many others, men of zeal and goodness, who have left their impress upon the Church.

Just as the Methodists possessed Charles and John Wesley, so Evangelicalism found its hymn-writers. John Newton, a converted sea captain, became curate of Olney in Buckinghamshire in 1764. His adventures in early life are wellnigh incredible. He had been slave-trader, and for a year a slave himself, companion of thieves and pirates, living amidst every imaginable form of vice. Yet in these surroundings he retained enough self-respect to learn Euclid and Latin; and when he came to himself the Bishop of Lincoln was with difficulty persuaded to ordain him. But his conversion had been real, and he set to work with extraordinary earnestness. About that time William Cowper, the poet, settled at Olney for the sake of his health, and Newton and he became friends. From these two proceeded many hymns that are now known and valued throughout the whole Church. "How Sweet the Name of Jesus Sounds" and "Glorious Things of Thee are Spoken" are Newton's, while Cowper wrote "O for a Closer Walk with God," "Hark, my soul! it is the Lord" and "Jesus, Where'er Thy People Meet," with many others.

Another Evangelical who cannot be omitted from even a brief account is Charles Simeon of Cambridge. The story is that he came up from Eton a careless youth, but, discovering that at King's he was expected to receive the Holy Communion, and realising that this was a serious thing, he bought a small book, *Bishop Wilson on the Lord's Supper,* and read it carefully. This changed his life. He took Holy Orders and laboured in Cambridge as an Evangelical, at first against great obstacles. But when he became known and trusted his influence was immense. He felt that the system of patronage, which deprived many of the Evangelical clergy of what he regarded as their due preferment, needed correction. So he used his private fortune to buy livings, forming the beginning of the Simeon Trust, which now owns over a hundred of them, including some of the most important in the country. Evangelical teaching in the Church was thus assured of continuance. In its early form, in spite of its piety and good works, which no observer can fail to recognise, it was somewhat detached from the main current of the Church's life, valuing too lightly, one feels, the historical continuity of the Church and the need for ordered and artistic expression of the common religious life in worship. We must not despise, either, the religion which consists in a quiet performance of duties and is suspicious of exciting " conversions." The great Church can find room for men of both types, providing they will respect each other. But since the Oxford Movement the best Catholics in the Church of England have learned to become Evangelical, and the best Evangelicals to-day are by no means lacking in the Catholic spirit.

CHAPTER VI

LIBERAL EVANGELICALISM

If you look in the Church papers, among the advertisements for clergy you will often find the description " Liberal Evangelical." Even where the adjective is not mentioned it is often implied. For Evangelicals of the old type, such as originated and continued the great Movement, are now rare, if they exist at all. Times have changed, and we have changed with them. How odd it would look to see Charles Simeon walking through the streets of Cambridge!

True, we still sing the Evangelical hymns; but do we write them? I think not. And we sing them with a difference. How far does a modern congregation enter into the spirit of words like these:

> " Rock of ages, cleft for me,
>   Let me hide myself in Thee ";

or—

> " Hide me, O my Saviour, hide,
>   Till the storm of life be past "?

It would be a bad day for religion, I freely admit, if it ever happened that such words awakened no responsive emotion in our hearts. But to-day they do not, and cannot, provide the main part of our spiritual sustenance, as they used to do. Other needs have entered in, and we see the world, our own destinies and God too with different eyes.

When I hear of " Abide with Me " being sung by tens of thousands at a Cup Final, I know not whether to weep or rejoice. Thank God for evidence of elemental needs in the human soul! But this unthinking surrender to mere emotionalism, is it likely to brace or to relax the spirit? How many would find that these words, being the simple expression of a life lived with God, nerved them to face death unafraid, as they did Henry Francis Lyte? One seems to hear the Communist whispering : " I told you religion was dope."

No : times have indeed changed, and our thoughts too. Men speak sarcastically of " hymns on death for dying men " which our fathers sang; and our latest hymn-book is called *Songs of Praise*. It is impossible for us to project our interests so wholly into the next life as it used to be. We place more value on present happenings, and the hymns we now compose are about the " City of God," poor men and rich men, justice and freedom, and so on. Simeon might tell us that we needed conversion, but we feel that the Spirit of God is leading us this way.

So now we have the Liberal Evangelicals, whose aim is to keep the spirit of their great predecessors and yet to have a message that men can understand to-day. They are a large and important section of the Church; if not so much numerically, at least in power and influence. Names like Vernon Storr, Guy Rogers, the Bishop of Croydon, and the new Bishop of Truro are representative of them. They probably enjoy more popularity than any other school, and from their ranks come bishops and other dignitaries. Dr. Inge has always asserted his preference for this school of thought, although he is himself an enigmatic personage, who would not easily fit into any group.

In what does their " liberalism " consist? First and foremost, I suppose, in a changed attitude to the Scriptures. There are individual differences here, of course, some going farther than others in the acceptance of the results of biblical study. The reader will be aware that the past fifty years has seen an enormous amount of investigation of the books of the Bible, so that we now know far more about them, when and how they were written, and the meaning the various writers intended their words to bear, than any Christians have done since the second century. Not that all problems are settled, or ever will be; but certain guiding lines are clear for all who have eyes to see. We know, for instance, that St. Mark's was the earliest of our four Gospels to be written. We know that the authors of St. Matthew and St. Luke both used St. Mark, making it a basis for their work, and adding other materials, either from living tradition or from early books which have now been lost. This knowledge greatly helps us to understand the meaning of the Gospels. It has been taught to all the clergy in Universities and Theological Colleges of any standing for nearly fifty years past; and I take it that " liberal " Evangelicals welcome this new knowledge, which frees us from the blind acceptance of every word of the Authorised Version, miscalled " fundamentalism." Wrong understanding of the Bible has given rise to wrong ideas of the character of God, and of Christ's person and work, which are largely responsible for the present neglect of religion. When the Church learns how to use the fuller knowledge she now possesses, her appeal will carry far more weight. But false doctrines die hard, and all true liberalism is to be welcomed.

I think, too, that I should not be wrong in ascribing to the newer Evangelicals a keener interest in the affairs of this life than their fathers had. In the old Evangelical preaching, as I remember it quite well in my own boyhood, salvation meant escaping hell and going to heaven when you died. I am sure of this, for I was greatly afraid of hell. It was fresh news to me, and an intense relief, when I first heard of the Catholic Church, which was God's society in this world, trying to make His will prevail in all things. Incidentally, Henry Scott Holland was the man from whom I learned most, the greatest and most charming preacher and writer I remember, who gave inspiration to thousands of young people through the Christian Social Union and the *Commonwealth Magazine*. What he and his fellow-workers taught is now the common possession of the Church. But this is by the way.

We must not forget the efforts of the great Evangelicals to free the slaves, help prisoners and improve conditions of work in factories. But after them came a generation less sensitive to social

3

ills, who were inclined to allow a few pious expressions to blind their eyes to much wickedness. These Evangelicals were for the most part well-to-do people, who had never questioned their right to their own luxuries, or the duty of the poor to be content with their lot.

> " The rich man in his castle,
> The poor man at his gate;
> God made them, high or lowly,
> And ordered their estate."

The words read quaintly to-day, and I suppose that Liberal Evangelicals, like most other men, would not dare to make God responsible for the Feudal System.

There was also a narrowness of mind in regard to innocent pleasures, such as dancing and the theatre. These were counted wicked, as was any amusement whatever on Sunday. Religion thus retreated into a pious shell of its own, where it could avoid contact with the wicked world. This was a deplorable thing; and, try as we will, we cannot now bridge the gulf then made, and claim all art and recreation as gracious gifts of our Father for His children's enjoyment, to be used as in His sight, and not shunned. " The evil that men do lives after them," said Shakespeare; and here is an example. Liberal Evangelicals would certainly plead for a humaner type of religion. We may hope that one day men will understand that God is not only the author of moral rules and the solemnities of worship, but also the inspirer of the joy of life and of all gladness and beauty.

As for doctrine, Liberal Evangelicals have given up the crude and harsh notions of the Atonement, which were once held, and tend, I should suppose, to think of the Atonement not by itself, but as one aspect of the wider fact of the Incarnation. There is indeed a greater measure of agreement on all doctrinal matters in the Church than there used to be. So much is this the case that Liberal Evangelicals often call themselves " Central Church men," although the old-fashioned High Churchman has at least an equal claim to this title. Whether it is good to be in the centre, and not on the wings, I will not presume to say! The fear of ceremonial, too, has practically vanished, and in many an Evangelical church one may see a simple yet dignified ceremonial on traditional English lines.

One weakness of Evangelicalism, as of Protestantism generally, has been its vagueness of doctrine about the Church. "Protestantism," says Dr. Visser 't Hooft, himself a Protestant, "has never taken the Church seriously." The Liberal Evangelicals at the present moment are more inclined than the Catholic section of the Church to make sacrifices, or departures from tradition, in order to come to an agreement with Free Churchmen. It is a difficult question. The Church is essential to Christianity, and probably to the very existence of religion. But on what principles is the Church based, and must its structure be the same everywhere? A formulation of Evangelical doctrine on this point, taking into account history and the New Testament, and universal in its scope—for a Church that cannot be universal is not Christian—is badly needed. Evangelicalism, however, has never been strong in theology. And the times are not entirely propitious. For men to-day are impatient of serious thought.

CHAPTER VII

MODERNISM

MODERNISM is often used as an epithet to hurl at somebody whose religious opinions you do not agree with. Yet in itself Modernism does not imply any particular doctrines. It is, according to M. Sabatier, "an orientation"—that is, a spirit or mental disposition. Consequently it has little organisation, has never been a "movement," in the sense of the Evangelical or Oxford Movements, and will never celebrate a centenary. Modernists point to men like Origen, Abelard and Erasmus, who, according to them, were Modernists in relation to the ages in which they lived. Some would even say that Christianity itself may be described as a modernistic expansion and re-interpretation of Judaism.

Nevertheless Modernism, as we know it to-day, has a story, if not a history. There are two chapters to the story—one concerned with the Church of Rome, the other with the Church of England. The first chapter is closed and sealed up; the second continues indefinitely.

In the nineteenth century a great struggle went on within the Church of Rome, between those who wanted the Church to be the pioneer in the fight for political and intellectual freedom, and those who dreaded the results of such a movement and preferred that the Church should make her own power secure and then resist change to the uttermost. The reformers were beaten. In 1864 a famous *Syllabus of Errors* was issued from Rome, among the errors being toleration of religious opinions, and "progress, liberalism and civilisation as lately introduced." In 1870 the Dogma of Papal Infallibility was decreed, and Rome set herself definitely against advances in knowledge or changes in human society.

Nevertheless thinking went on. In 1878 was founded the Catholic Institute of Paris, among its professors being Louis Duchesne, a young scholar already known for his wide knowledge and independent judgment. Three years later Alfred Loisy, one of his pupils, became professor of Hebrew at the Institute. Both these men believed that in their studies, one of Church History and the other of the Bible, scientific methods should be employed, and that efforts should be made to discover the actual truth, whether this agreed with previous opinions or not. Early Church history, as Duchesne found it, was a different thing from the history commonly believed by pious Romanists; and Loisy found contradictions between scientific teaching and the book of Genesis. Much of this is commonplace now, but it was not so then. In the Church of England, if we discover that our forefathers made a mistake about Genesis, we can correct the mistake. But how could a Church with an infallible head admit mistakes? Duchesne and Loisy got over this difficulty by saying that what was not strictly true in history might yet be suitable material for faith and edification. This caused much opposition. Duchesne was suspended for a year; but Loisy was able to continue, somewhat precariously, till 1892.

In 1893 Rome issued an encyclical *Providentissimus Deus*, condemning " disquieting tendencies " in Biblical interpretation, which, if they prevailed, could not fail " to destroy the inspired and supernatural character of the Bible." This was under Leo XIII., a cautious man, and not wholly obscurantist. Pius X., who succeeded him in 1903, was of a different temper. He would not admit that a jot of the Catholic tradition was untrue or imperfect.

Now Harnack, the Liberal Protestant of Germany, had been saying that the essence of Christianity was the proclamation of the Fatherhood of God by Jesus. Everything else—Church, creeds, sacraments—had grown around this. Harnack believed that by his researches he could trace the process of growth. Loisy too had to admit, as any candid student must, that there had been much growth. It was absurd to say that the Roman Church of 1900 was precisely the same as the Church on the Day of Pentecost. The New Testament was not completed till 100 A.D., and the Creeds not till 451 A.D. How, then, could he oppose Harnack, who inferred that all this additional material, much of it common to Protestants and Catholics, was not essential to Christianity?

Loisy wrote a little book, *The Gospel and the Church*, in defence of the Roman Catholic position. He admitted the growth but he called it development. Newman had written his Essay on *Development* long before this to meet the same difficulty. He felt that all Roman developments were present in the apostolic faith, though the Apostles were not aware of them. It was something like the picture on a photographic plate, which is there all the time, but only becomes evident when it is wanted. Loisy was more radical than Newman. He compared Christianity to a living seed, which does actually grow, clothing itself with a body suitable to its environment—that is to say, adopting an organised form, a creed, and all the rest of it, to enable men to understand and appropriate its essence. No seed could survive apart from this. " To blame the Catholic Church for having developed its constitution," said Loisy, " is to blame it for having lived."

The trouble is that this explanation, though clearly useful within limits, may be used to justify any development whatever. It offers no means of distinguishing between true development and perversion of the original life. But Pius X. did not condemn it on that ground. For he was not prepared to submit the New Testament and the history of the Church to candid examination, confident that the truth in them needed no external authority to bolster it up. He feared whither the new methods would lead, and so Loisy was excommunicated, his books banned and the movement effectually repressed.

Those who think the Pope was right may take comfort in this, that recently Loisy, now an old man, has published his *Birth of*

Christianity, in which he represents our Lord as a simple peasant, of no great character or originality, obsessed by the same apocalyptic dreams which filled the minds of so many of His contemporaries. But we must remember that Loisy has been cut off from the Church for many years. This may have helped his mind to proceed to such perverse and unnecessary extremes. The Modernist condemnation, too, included other men of more reasonable opinions, men who cared deeply for truth and saw the need for reform in Roman theology. Von Hügel, being a layman, was left alone, and all Christians are debtors to him. George Tyrrell's name is well known. I remember reading his books as they came out. No one can learn his story without being drawn to love him. It could scarcely be necessary for the true Church to cast out such children.

In the Church of England, as I said, we need not refuse to examine new knowledge when it is presented to us. We are slow, naturally and rightly, in admitting new ideas, but we do not, as a rule, persecute our advanced thinkers. Roman Modernism has had little direct effect upon us. Liberal thought of a modern type may be said to begin in the Church of England by the publication of *Essays and Reviews* in 1860. Where Scripture was in conflict with science, the writers contended, the scriptural theory must be abandoned, as in the accounts of the Creation in Genesis. Benjamin Jowett argued that the Bible should be interpreted like any other book. Powell said that " if miracles were in the estimation of a former age among the chief supports of Christianity they are at present among its main difficulties." The general tone of the book was negative, and it was received with much hostility. In 1864 a Declaration, signed by 11,000 clergy and 137,000 laity, was presented to the Archbishop at Lambeth affirming the inspiration and divine authority of the Bible, without reserve or qualification, and the doctrine of everlasting punishment. But, owing chiefly to the Privy Council, nothing serious happened to the writers of the *Reviews*.

About this time occurred the Colenso case in South Africa.

Bishop Colenso wrote a work on the Pentateuch in which he denied the Mosaic authorship, and asserted that Joshua was a mythical character, and that there were two incompatible accounts of the Creation and the Flood. Here, again, it was not so much what Colenso said, as the bald and abrupt manner of his saying it. People were not ready for such doctrine, and still less for Colenso's suggestion that God's punishments may be remedial, leading at last to salvation for all. Although the Privy Council supported Colenso, most of the South African bishops and clergy were against him and he was condemned for heresy. This resulted in a schism in South Africa, which is still not completely healed.

In spite of the general disapproval with which these new opinions were met, a Royal Commission in 1864 recommended that the clergy in future should not be bound by every word of the Thirty-Nine Articles, but should " assent " to them in their general tenor and meaning, and an Act was passed to this effect.

English Modernism is for the most part of a Protestant rather than a Catholic sort. Yet the most notable contribution to modern thought has come from the Catholic side. In 1889 was published *Lux Mundi*, by a group of young men, most of whom afterwards occupied high positions in the Church. Times had altered since 1860, and many of the clergy were relieved to find ways by which the old faith and new knowledge could be reconciled. Charles Gore's essay on *Inspiration*, in which he pictured the Bible as recording a progressive revelation of God, and not necessarily accurate in every detail, attracted most attention. No serious scholarship has since gone back on Gore's position. The Church as a whole has been exceedingly rich in men of modern outlook, who can face problems and welcome inquiry while retaining their faith.

But the most definite and widely known Modernism is that represented by the Modern Churchmen's Union, of which the Bishop of Birmingham, Dr. Inge and Dr. Major are outstanding members. Their thought is mainly critical and destructive;

not the less necessary for that, perhaps, for there are many errors to be removed from the popular mind. But soon a fresh theology, positive and constructive, will be needed; one which will take full account of new knowledge about the Bible, the Church, Man and the Universe. For this the experience and co-operation of all types of mind in the Church will be called for.

Our Lord compared the scribe who had entered the kingdom of heaven to a householder " who bringeth forth out of his treasures things new and old." The old is the Church tradition, not to be despised; the new is fresh truth, not to be rejected. Somehow we must combine them, and the effort, though difficult, is the very life-blood of religion.

CHAPTER VIII

THE ROMAN CATHOLIC CHURCH

I

THE clergy continually hear the complaint that whereas Roman Catholics understand the history of their Church, most churchmen are wholly ignorant of the true character of the Church of England. "A man in the office said to-day," one will tell us, "that the Church of England began in the reign of Henry the Eighth and is no true church at all. He seemed to know his facts, and I could not tell how to answer him."

To make things clearer for those in like difficulties, I propose to explain how the Roman Catholic Church became what it is. This will involve a little history, but readers must be patient with that, for there is no way of understanding the problem except by knowing the history. In the next chapter I shall deal with the present claims of the Roman Church and their validity.

"After I have been there," said St. Paul, "I must also see Rome." Why? Because Rome was then the centre of the world, and neither St. Paul nor anyone else could foresee a time when this would not be so. In the second and third centuries Rome became the focus of the active Church in the West. It was not the centre of the whole Church, for Jerusalem, Ephesus, Antioch and Alexandria were flourishing homes of Christianity, entirely independent of Rome. Nor was the Bishop of Rome head of the Church. This claim was never made, nor would it have been accepted, or even understood in the East, if it had been made.

But in the West Rome undoubtedly had a pre-eminence, due to its central position and the wisdom and courage of a long succession of bishops. It formed a natural court of appeal in case of disputes. It was a missionary Church, throwing out branches in North Africa, Gaul, Germany, Spain and Britain. Over these Churches it exercised a benevolent supervision, quite rightly and inevitably. When in the time of St. Cyprian, about 250 A.D., the Bishop of Rome claimed more he was sharply resisted. St. Cyprian's theory was that the Church was governed by bishops and that each of these was theoretically equal; a primacy of honour, however, might be allowed to the Bishop of Rome owing to the importance of his See. The Eastern Churches were entirely unconcerned with this dispute.

There was then, and has always remained, a difference of feeling and outlook between the Church of the West, looking to Rome as its mother, and the Churches of the East, each autonomous, having no clear centre, but loosely federated for common action when such was necessary. Rome, though its earliest services were in Greek, was Latin in temperament. Quite early it produced a simple creed, which has come down to us as the Apostles' Creed. The Eastern Churches developed a different statement of faith, longer and more philosophical. This, after many changes, was accepted by Rome and has become universal under the name of the Nicene Creed. But the Roman Creed was never used in the East, nor is it used to this day.

As soon as persecution relaxed, Christians built themselves churches in which their sacred rites, Baptism and the Eucharist, could be performed. The services had been simple and free at the very first, but soon acquired definite form. It is a mistake to think that the Christian rites were originally performed anyhow, without ceremony or dignity. Symbolism, such as that of lights, and vestments to distinguish bishop or priest or singers, are a natural accompaniment of Christian worship. The southern peoples may carry these things to a degree of elaborateness not wholly to our northern taste, but the principle is rooted in Christian history. The Quaker assembly, with its absence of art and order and ceremony, may or may not be desirable, but it is certainly an innovation and not a return to early custom.

Consequently, at the beginning of the fourth century the Christian Church was firmly rooted in all the lands round the Mediterranean, with outposts in Britain, Germany, on the Danube and in Southern Russia. Everywhere Christian worship was framed on similar lines and would have looked much the same to a stranger observing it. In matters of faith and administration Rome had a certain pre-eminence in the West, but none whatever in the East.

Early in the fourth century two vital events occurred. Persecution ceased, and the Church was free to live its life without fear or restraint. And, more important still, Constantine removed the centre of the Empire from Rome to his new city of Constantinople. For long Rome had been out of touch with the Eastern parts of the Empire, and the Emperors were no longer Romans in the old sense of that word. At one blow Rome was dethroned from its venerable supremacy. The Emperors lived in the East, and cared little for Italy. But an unforeseen result occurred. As the Imperial power declined in the West, so the Bishop of Rome gradually became the most important personage there. When at the end of the fourth century the barbarians began to pour over the Alps on to the fertile lands of Italy, the Emperor at Constantinople was too far away to repel them. The power in Italy which met the invaders, treated with them and finally converted them to orthodox Christianity—for most of them were already Arians—was the power of the Bishop of Rome.

It was at this period that the real Papacy was born, not by fraud or scheming, but by the logic of events. The old Roman world in the West had crumbled, and the new was not yet formed. But after several centuries of struggle and darkness a new power arose in France and Germany, which promised to restore the Roman culture almost lost in the dark ages. Charles the Great, the Frankish King, came to Rome and attended Mass in St. Peter's on Christmas Day, 800, with his court. At the close of the service Pope Leo III. placed a golden crown on his head and proclaimed him Cæsar Augustus, the successor of the old Roman Emperors. The Popes had already obtained from Charles's father the grant of Italian lands known as the " States of the Church." This gave them wealth and the prestige of temporal power.

Thus originated the Holy Roman Empire, ruled by two twin powers, the Emperor in temporal and the Pope in spiritual matters. During the middle ages there was constant friction between the two, each desiring to be supreme. The rights and wrongs of the quarrel are hard to determine. On the one hand, it seems incongruous that the representative of Him who said, " My kingdom is not of this world," should own territories, direct armies, possess enormous wealth and plot and plan just as worldly sovereigns do. On the other hand, if the Church has to live in this world it can hardly help accommodating itself, in a measure, to its surroundings. We may perhaps admit, with hesitation, that the Papacy was justifiable in the ages that called for it. It only became wrong when the need for it had passed away. But the Roman Pontiffs, having once tasted power, have never been willing to give it up.

No one can understand why Rome to-day claims religious sovereignty, universal and absolute, unless he bears in mind this history. Rome never forgets that she was once supreme in Western Europe. She seeks to recover and extend that supremacy. All this has no more to do with Christianity than have the title-deeds of Lambeth Palace or the architecture of Westminster Abbey. Rome turns temporary accidents into permanent essentials.

The ordinary convert to Rome knows little about Church history, and cares less. He joins the Roman Church because he is told that Christ gave the headship over the Church to St. Peter, who became Bishop of Rome and transmitted his powers to his successors until the end of time. But this argument was framed to account for and justify what had already happened. In the same way the latest articles of the Roman faith, the Immaculate Conception and the Infallibility of the Pope, are designed to buttress a position already occupied for other reasons; the last one, indeed, if accepted, makes the position impregnable.

After the coming of Augustine to England in 597 the Church in England, which had previously been British and independent, passed under the leadership of Rome. We need not regret this. Rome had much to teach our people. The position is the same as that in the mission field to-day, where we support and direct native Churches until they are strong enough to stand on their own feet. The ideal is that they should be independent, joined to us by ties of love and a common faith, not of submission to an overlord. Rome's first relation to England was of this Christian character, but as the Popes changed from bishops into temporal rulers, so they treated the Church of England as a vassal rather than a sister Church. The English were always restless under this, as history clearly shows. When the Reformation split came, it was not a sudden affair, but the culmination of differences which had been growing greater ever since the Norman Conquest.

II

In the last section I explained how the Church of Rome obtained its pre-eminence in Western Europe in medieval times. At the Reformation this pre-eminence was challenged, and most of the northern peoples rejected it. But the southern peoples, whose life had been more deeply influenced by the Latin culture, remained constant. They could not understand religion apart from Rome any more than the Jew of old could understand it apart from Jerusalem.

The break between the old and the new was less marked in England than in Germany or Scandinavia. The English dislike revolutions, preferring where they can to graft the new on to the old and to retain all that seems valuable of the past. Consequently England presents the spectacle, unique in Western Europe, of a Catholic Church independent of Rome.

In this connexion I should like to refer the thoughtful reader to a recent book entitled, *Anglo-Catholicism and Orthodoxy*, by Dr. Visser 't Hooft, General Secretary of the World Student

Christian Federation. Dr. Hooft, like most Continental Protestants, at first believed that the Church of England was just another variety of Protestantism, akin to their own Churches. But experience has taught him that we have in England something quite different from these. And since our Non-Roman Catholicism is rapidly encircling the globe in the immense Anglican Communion, and at the same time entering into friendly relations with the orthodox Churches of the East, Dr. Hooft sees in it a fact of major importance for the future of Christianity. The book is well worth reading for its wide knowledge, its impartiality and its statesmanlike grasp of realities.

Since the Reformation the Roman Church has made continuous efforts to bring the Church of England once again under its sway. At first there was a possibility that this might come about through a restoration of the Stuarts to the Crown of England. But the English people went so far as to prefer kings from Holland and Germany, whom they liked but little, to Stuarts, whom they liked much better, but whose rule would have involved a return to the Roman obedience. So religious propaganda was intensified, and in 1850 England was divided by Pius IX. into fresh dioceses, to which Roman bishops were appointed, as if the Church of England had no existence. This movement has culminated in the building of the magnificent cathedral at Westminster and the commencement of another at Liverpool. The ministry needed for this direct and widespread attack on the Church of England is drawn chiefly from Ireland and the Continent.

The arguments used to justify the Roman position are as follows:

(i.) That St. Peter was appointed by our Lord Prince of the Apostles and Ruler of the Church.

(ii.) That he went to Rome and ruled there as bishop for twenty-five years until his martyrdom.

(iii.) That his office and powers were intended to be handed on to his successors in the See of Rome.

Neither of these propositions can be proved. Taken as they stand, the first two can be definitely disproved. The third is an inference from the others, but not a necessary inference; it can neither be proved nor disproved. The propositions form a chain, in which each depends on the rest. If only one is untrue the Roman case falls to the ground. On the other hand, if all were true they would not be sufficient to justify the domineering attitude of Rome towards Christians outside its own borders. There are other forms of leadership besides the autocracy of the Roman pontiffs.

The first proposition rests upon our Lord's words in St. Matthew xvi. 18-19 : " And I also say unto thee, that thou art Peter, and upon this rock I will build my church; and the gates of Hades shall not prevail against it. I will give unto thee the keys of the kingdom of heaven : and whatsoever thou shalt bind on earth shall be bound in heaven : and whatsoever thou shalt loose on earth shall be loosed in heaven."

Now everyone knows that volumes have been written on the interpretation of these words. Here I can only make three brief comments. First, it is St. Peter as a man of faith upon whom our Lord says He can build His Church. Why may not other men of like faith equally prove rocks upon which He can build? Look carefully, and you will see that nothing whatever is said about St. Peter's being supreme over his brethren. Our Lord makes certain assertions about him; but we must not assume that He makes analogous denials about everyone else.

Secondly, our Lord spoke in poetic language, with rich imagery. The Latin mind is wont to take a passage like this as if it were a legal document, to be laboriously interpreted letter for letter. To a lawyer words such as " keys " and " binding " or " loosing " suggest the ideas of possession, domination and exclusion; but these are not the only meanings they can convey. The Gospel is a gospel of freedom, and faith in Christ is indeed a key which leads us into the larger land of the Kingdom of God.

Thirdly, if our Lord had meant to make St. Peter pre-eminent among the Apostles, it is astonishing that no hint of it appears elsewhere in the New Testament. St. James, "the Lord's brother," is head of the Jerusalem Council, even though St. Peter is present. Just before the Passion, St. James and St. John ask for the first place in the kingdom that was coming (St. Mark x. 35-45). They seem quite unaware that this has already been promised to St. Peter. Whether the kingdom was to be on earth or in heaven makes little difference here. If St. Peter had been recognised as pre-eminent among the Twelve the request of St. James and St. John could never have been made. St. Paul asserts that he was entrusted with the mission to the Gentiles, and that St. Peter's work was confined to Jews.

As for the injunction to St. Peter in St. John xxi., "Feed my sheep," which the Romanists also bring forward in support of their case, this is plainly the restoration of a fallen apostle to his former office. The passage neither asserts nor implies that he should take precedence over his fellow-apostles.

In regard to the second proposition there is no proof that St. Peter was ever in Rome. By proof I mean something equivalent to Acts xxviii., which describes the entry of St. Paul into that city. But there is an early and persistent tradition that St. Peter was there, and as this is not likely to have arisen out of nothing we may accept it as true. He was not, however, at Rome when St. Paul wrote his Epistle to the Romans (about 56 A.D.); if he had been, it is incredible that St. Paul should not have referred to the fact. And when St. Paul reached Rome in 59 A.D., and remained there a prisoner for two years, there is no mention of St. Peter being in the city. If, therefore, he ever went to Rome, it could only have been for a short time before his death. No doubt the Roman Christians were very proud to have had among them, even for a short while, the great Apostle who had been a companion of our Lord in His earthly ministry. After his martyrdom they would make the most of this connexion. But the story of St. Peter's twenty-five-years' episcopate at Rome is the imaginative invention of a later age.

The third proposition will fall with the second. But to-day there are many people, including probably not a few Roman Catholic scholars, who, although they know that the stories about St. Peter are unhistorical, yet maintain that our Lord must have appointed some authority to rule His Church and to declare His will. Otherwise, they think, uncertainty and anarchy would result; and as an example they point to Protestantism, which, for want of a visible head, has split into innumerable fragments. Many people to-day join the Church of Rome on this ground alone, that it is the only Christian body which speaks with a single authoritative and infallible voice. It is the same impulse which, in political life, is leading men to distrust their own powers and to seek shelter under the wing of some all-powerful dictator.

But the Gospel is meant to give men life, not security. The price paid for such security is the loss of personality. Autocracies turn men into automata, things that can be trusted to think and behave exactly as they are told. Jesus Christ came to quicken our personality, not to deaden it; and those who believe that His spirit dwells with us can have confidence that, in spite of our perplexities and divisions, we are seeking after, and shall one day attain, a richer unity than the legal and mechanical one which Rome offers, a unity that shall respect our personality and not be afraid of the truth.

III

A friend of mine, a parish priest, tells me that he is often in trouble with a few of his parishioners because he wishes to introduce small items of ceremonial to which they are unaccustomed. They think he is " going to Rome." " And yet," he adds, " I am really farther away from Rome than any other person in the parish." Herein lies not only a truth, but a warning. English churchmen who oppose Rome *for the wrong reasons* are always in danger of finding out their error; and when they do, their opposition collapses like a house of cards. It is well known that large numbers of Rome's recruits come from strongly Protestant families. Bring up a child to believe that there is something wicked in wearing a vestment, and (who knows?) one day he may find himself Mayor of a borough, or a high Freemason, clad in scarves and aprons and wearing danglums round his neck. He may then conclude that symbolism which is natural to express civic dignity or fraternal loyalty is just as natural to express our sense of God's majesty, before whom the Saints wear white robes and carry palms and the elders fall low on their faces in worship. If, when he has awakened to this truth, he finds his parish church cold, bare, and perhaps ugly into the bargain, he may walk through the first Roman church door that he finds open without troubling much about Pope or the niceties of creeds. A hungry man eats the first meal he can get.

In the previous sections I tried to indicate the true reasons why we should oppose the Church of Rome. Her claim to universal dominion finds no support either in the Bible or in Church history. Moreover, it is out of harmony with the spirit of Christ, who did not die under Pontius Pilate in order to found another empire even more intolerant than that of ancient Rome. "The kings of the Gentiles exercise lordship," He said, "but it shall not be so among you." And even if the people of Italy or Spain or Ireland prefer the Papal form of Church government to any other, that is no reason why the Roman Church should enter England, where the Papacy was rejected four centuries ago, and try by every means to seduce our people from their natural allegiance.

Having these reasons clearly in our mind, we ought to be ready to recognise the many fine qualities of Roman Catholic religion and worship. Take, for instance, this question of ceremonial. There are some people, like the Quakers, who seem temperamentally averse to all ceremonial. But they are, and will ever remain, a small body. For ordinary men all corporate life demands ceremony. Look at the Army and the Navy, the Judges,

Parliament, and any civic or commercial association you can
think of, and you will find that men, when moved by one
dominating idea or engaged in any serious common task, fashion
for themselves an elaborate mode of doing it. This proceeding
gives, so they believe, dignity to their acts and lifts them out of
the level of everyday life. I remember how this truth was impressed upon me many years ago, when as a young man I read
Carlyle's *Sartor Resartus*. I suppose nobody reads Carlyle now,
and yet I doubt whether Wells and Huxley and the modern
coterie of " intellectuals " have so much to teach us as the shrewd
old sage of Chelsea.

The Roman Church is a very old Church and she has learned
much in her long history. Most of her services, and the Mass
pre-eminently, are so framed as to respond to this human desire
for beauty and dignity. To our northern notions, however, her
ceremonial seems over-elaborate, fussy and often meaningless.
At the Reformation our Prayer Book was meant not to abolish
ceremonies but to simplify them and make them intelligible to
all the worshippers. Unfortunately, in practice the reaction
against ceremonial went too far. Cromwell angrily exclaimed,
" Take away that bauble," when he saw the mace in the House of
Commons; and his Puritan followers broke the windows and
defaced the statues in many a church and cathedral, with results
which we are trying to repair at great expense to-day. A corresponding reaction in the forms of our worship kept our services
much less warm and beautiful than the Prayer Book meant them
to be. This did not matter so much during the dull days of the
eighteenth century; but when the Romantic revival began early
in the nineteenth we were at a great disadvantage as compared
with Rome. The Oxford Movement tried to remedy this, but
often by the unfortunate method of copying Roman ceremonial,
since the sound English traditions had been largely forgotten.
We live in happier times now, when there is not only a more
widespread demand for beauty in worship, but wise guidance as
to the methods of providing it. No intelligent person should,

therefore, any longer imagine that the desire for ceremonial has anything to do with Romanism.

Another mistake is the complacent way in which we surrender the title " Catholic " to the Romanists. It is inexplicable that men who declare Sunday by Sunday their belief in the " Holy Catholic Church " should act and speak in public as if Romanists were the only " Catholics." Early education has much to do with it, for until recently our school history books were written by men who had no understanding of the Church of England. But the Church herself acquiesced far too long in this error. Certainly in official statements we are now more careful to insist on our lawful heritage. It will not delay the day of reunion but, in my judgment, will bring it appreciably nearer, when all churchpeople boldly claim the name of Catholic for themselves and their parish churches, as the Prayer Book gives them every right to do.

And do not let us confuse Catholicism with the Invocation of Saints or with an excessive veneration for our Lord's holy Mother. These are practices added to the primitive faith by the Church of Rome. Any reader can see that they were unknown in New Testament times. I am sure that St. Paul would have been greatly shocked to hear of them. They would have drawn from him another letter like the Epistle to the Galatians. But they are not negations of the Christian spirit, such as the claim to universal domination is. They are simply exaggerations of tendencies which to some people, especially those of Southern Europe, appear natural and harmless. They arise from popular devotion, which even Popes and theologians cannot control. The religion of the Prayer Book is of an austerer sort; yet it contains all the essentials for a true Catholic life, and if we use it to the full we shall find that it supplies the needs of the soul in every mood and through every experience.

Churchpeople often believe that the Church of Rome is a paradise in which no differences of opinion are to be found, but every member is loyal in the support of his Church and the performance of his duties. They contrast this with our controversies and our lax discipline. But the whole idea is legendary. Rome has its own difficulties. In many of the Catholic countries she is faced by masses of secularist opinion, created largely through her own policy, and bitterly opposed to religion in every shape or form. We have nothing comparable to it in England. And Romanists in general are no more angels than Anglicans are, although Rome has a more penetrating knowledge of human nature than we have, and knows better how to deal with imperfect people. Read between the lines in the *Tablet*, and you will often find evidence of turmoil beneath the apparently calm waters of Romanist life. Or take a recent book, such as *A Catholic Plea for Reunion*, by Father Jerome, and see how far off the beaten track a Roman priest's thoughts sometimes stray. And what one man dares to write many others are certainly thinking.

Keble exhorted us to " speak gently of our sister's fall." There is something priggish about that which is distasteful. We shall oppose her unalterably where she is wrong. But we shall acknowledge the vast services which she has performed, and is still performing, for mankind. I do not see why we should even mind learning from her to be a little less insular, a little more universal. The world moves fast to-day. Perhaps understanding, and reunion, are nearer than we suppose.

CHAPTER IX

THE EASTERN ORTHODOX CHURCH

I

FIFTY years ago few Englishmen had ever heard of the existence of these Churches. We were taught at school that Christians were divided into Catholics and Protestants, the former being the Roman Catholics and the latter most Englishmen and a good number of Germans. We were aware of the existence of countries like Russia and Greece, but these had nothing to do with the Reformation and did not come into our educational map so far as religion was concerned.

To-day all this is changed. The war, and the linking up of nations by modern invention and travel, have caused it to be generally known that there are great Churches in the East whose members are neither Romanists, nor Anglo-Catholics, nor Protestants. They call themselves Orthodox—that is, people who claim to hold the "correct belief," the unchanged traditional faith of the Church.

As I write I have before me a booklet issued by the Press and Publications Board of the Church Assembly entitled, *A Survey of the Affairs of the Orthodox Church*. Herein are enumerated no less than nine divisions of this Church—viz., the Patriarchate of Constantinople, the Church of Alexandria, the Patriarchate of Jerusalem, the Church of Cyprus, the Church of Rumania, the Church of Greece, the Serbian Church, the Church of Bulgaria, and the Russian Church. All these are self-governing Churches, and yet in communion with each other.

Observe at the outset a fundamental difference between these Churches and the Church of Rome. The latter has always aimed at a centralisation of Church government. She aspired to be an autocracy that should continue in a spiritual sense the universal jurisdiction of the Roman Empire. This plan fell to pieces at the Reformation, but Rome has not yet given up hopes of regaining her power. The Orthodox Churches, however, have never been within the Roman orbit. Historically they owe nothing to Rome, although Rome owes much to them. And just as they have never been under the dominion of Rome, so they have never wished to dominate one another, being content to live as sister Churches in a federation. They all look with respect to the Patriarch of Constantinople, whom they regard as their chief bishop, but in internal affairs each Church is completely independent. It is this characteristic which has made possible in recent years a closer understanding between them and the Church of England. Though our paths have differed so widely, we have many things in common. Unity is not yet achieved; but there are no such barriers, seemingly insurmountable, between us and the Orthodox as there are between us and Rome.

One of the many happy features of the marriage between our Prince George and Princess Marina has been that both bride and bridegroom can retain their ancestral faith and yet not feel estranged from one another in religion. The Princess is of the Orthodox faith, and an Orthodox ecclesiastic was present at the marriage in Westminster Abbey. Afterwards another ceremony was held, to perform the more elaborate rites of the Orthodox Church to which the Princess is naturally accustomed.

It is obvious that some of the Orthodox Churches are of great antiquity. All the Epistles of St. Paul, except that to the Romans, were written to Churches from which the present Orthodox Churches in those parts can trace an unbroken descent. At Jerusalem the continuity was broken from 70 A.D., when the original Jewish Christian Church was scattered just prior to the destruction of the city, until 135 A.D., when the Church became a Gentile one with Gentile bishops. Since then its history is continuous. We do not forget that the Church of Rome is equally ancient and continuous. But it can claim no precedence over these Churches of the East. Moreover, Rome itself was for nearly a hundred and fifty years a predominantly Greek Church, holding its services in Greek and officered by bishops who wrote and spoke in Greek. It was only when the Latin element became supreme that the claims of Rome to be mistress of the Christian world arose.

During the days of persecution—that is, up to 313 A.D.—these Churches—Jerusalem, Alexandria, Antioch, Ephesus and the like—were as free, as independent of each other, and as independent of Rome, as their successors are to-day. They were united in the essentials of the Faith, and they shared in the marvellous organisation whereby a Christian could make himself at home with brethren wherever he travelled, from Britain to the Euphrates; but there was no subservience. Naturally primacies of honour were recognised; Antioch, Alexandria and Rome being more highly regarded than smaller Churches. We should place the Bishop of London above the Bishop, say, of Southwell or Sodor and Man, but that does not mean that the one has power to order the other about, or more votes to cast in a Council. What strikes us about the Church of these early centuries is the extraordinary common sense of its arrangements. There was unity, and efficiency, combined with breadth and freedom. Certainly the Church had its quarrels and heresies, but it did not conquer the world by means of them. It was the massive wisdom, goodness and zeal displayed by countless Christians living a free, unfettered life which made the Church irresistible.

Let me give one instance, an unhappy dispute, to illustrate this spirit of independence. Early in the third century a young man named Origen, whose father had recently perished as a martyr, established a reputation as a teacher in the Church at Alexandria. No one like him, said St. Jerome long afterwards, had arisen in the Church since the days of the Apostles. But, owing to causes which I cannot go into here, but which were certainly not all the fault of Origen, he was excommunicated by his Bishop Demetrius, Patriarch of Alexandria. Demetrius communicated his decision to other bishops, including the Bishop of Rome, who endorsed it. But Theoctistus, Bishop of Cæsarea, who had welcomed Origen to his diocese, took no notice of Rome's condemnation. Origen taught at Cæsarea, and enjoyed vast popularity, from 231 A.D. till his death in 251 A.D., after torture and imprisonment in the persecution of Decius. At the Second Council of Constantinople in 553 A.D. he was condemned as a heretic; but by the Council, not the Pope, for Vigilius of Rome was not present.

A momentous change took place when Christianity was freed from persecution by Constantine. This Emperor found, as his immediate predecessors had done, that the East was a more congenial place to live and rule in than Rome. He transferred the seat of Empire to his new city of Constantinople, calling it New Rome to distinguish it from the old. A new church, dedicated to the Apostles of Christ, was erected, and a bishop appointed, who was to rank second to the Bishop of Old Rome. The rise of this new See was the occasion of much jealousy on the part of Alexandria, but the prestige afforded by the Imperial presence and government was sufficient to gain for it the highest place of honour among the Eastern Churches. Indeed, it soon claimed equality with Rome itself, and on no occasion did it ever admit the Roman supremacy. As Rome declined in political importance, owing to the absence of the emperors, so Constantinople grew. In the sixth century Justinian built there the magnificent Church of the Holy Wisdom (Latinised into St. Sophia), which still stands, although, alas! no longer in Christian hands.

II

During the first four centuries of Christian history—to be precise, up to 451 A.D.—the Greek Churches of the East performed for us a service for which we can never be too grateful.

They produced what we call the Nicene Creed, though in fact it was not completely formulated until the Council of Chalcedon in 451 A.D. This creed is typically Greek. The Latins were content with the short statement of faith which is called the Apostles' Creed. This is clear and definite, and taken wholly from Scripture. It tells us to believe in the Father, the Son and the Holy Ghost; but it goes no further. It assumes that we shall know that Father, Son and Holy Ghost are one God, not three, and that we either know, or do not curiously inquire, what are the relations existing between them. It is doubtful whether the Latin mind, left to itself, would ever have gone beyond this. But the Greeks persistently asked questions; and they had a long intellectual tradition behind them, going back before the Christian era to Plato, one of the great thinkers of the world. Hence arose much argument, and also, alas! many quarrels and excommunications. But finally the creed emerged which was accepted by the great majority of Christians, in East and West alike.

When next in some quiet morning hour you say the Nicene Creed, or, better still, sing it to Merbecke or some other manly and stirring tune such as it deserves, have a thought for these Greeks of long ago who hammered out for us this majestic hymn of our faith.

When once a question had been authoritatively settled the Latins were wont to regard further discussion upon it as impiety. To many of the Greeks, however, a settlement was only the beginning of fresh disputations. That was their weakness. The Latins need religion for practical purposes, for saving men from sin and its consequences. The Greeks need it for revealing the nature of God. For the first you must frame a system which, once well constructed, will serve for long, perhaps for ever. But the second has no end; for however much you think, there are always problems beyond you; and the danger is that discussion may become hair-splitting, and the serious issues of life may be forgotten in a flood of talk.

Although the Chalcedonian settlement was accepted nominally

by the whole Church, there were many in the East, especially in Egypt, who did not like it. For it said that Christ had two natures, one truly human and one truly divine, whereas they were accustomed to think of the human nature of Christ as being swallowed up in the divine, so that after the Incarnation only one nature really remained. They were therefore called Monophysites, or people who believed in the One Nature. So in the fifth century Egypt drifted apart from the West, and in Syria and Palestine bitter controversy ensued for centuries. Rome was too busy to attend to these questions. In Italy the barbarians were supplanting the old rulers, and the Popes had a great part to play in keeping the faith intact until they could convert these rude warriors, who were for the most part Christians, but of the imperfect Arian sort and poorly instructed at that. "In all history," says Dr. Foakes Jackson, "nothing is more remarkable than the way in which Latin Christianity fought and overcame the barbarism which engulfed the Empire." It was in these days that the Papacy was for the West a necessity, and we who object to it now that it is an anachronism ought to pay our tribute the more warmly to the great men who then occupied the See of Rome.

When a like trouble came to the East, as it soon did, no great leaders were there to stem the tide. Early in the seventh century Mohammed appeared as the prophet of a new religion among the Arabs. He felt that Christians worshipped several gods. It is not wholly to be wondered at that amid the babel of controversy then going on Mohammed failed to discern the true teaching of Christianity. But his mind was of a primitive Semitic sort, and he would probably have been incapable of appreciating the Christian faith in any form. For his religion was in fact a reaction to early Semitic ideas, as is shown by its admission of slavery and polygamy and its essentially warlike character. But it proved congenial to the hardy Arabs, who were beginning to expand and needed a leader and a cause to unite them and other lands in which to overflow. Egypt soon fell before these fierce invaders, and it is amazing to consider how within a century not only Syria and the whole of North Africa, but countries so far off as Spain, Persia and even India were conquered and had a new religion planted in their midst. Alexandria, Jerusalem and Antioch became Mohammedan cities, and the Churches there, once great and free, now represented the religion of a subject people.

Thus the Roman Empire in the East shrank to small proportions. But Constantinople still resisted. A Roman Emperor was to reign there for many centuries yet, with a free Christian Patriarch at his side. Try as they would the Arabs could not cross the narrow straits that separated Asia from Europe. But the western section of the conquerors passed into Spain and from thence attempted to reach Rome itself. Here, however, they met a different class of opponent from the degenerate Syrians and Egyptians. At a great battle near Tours in 732 they were defeated by Charles Martel, King of the Franks, and driven back into Spain. There they remained for centuries longer.

After the first shock of the Mohammedan conquests the Eastern Empire recovered itself under Leo the Isaurian in the eighth century. From this time onwards the Church and Empire at Constantinople were in close union. But the Church tended to become subordinate, a mere accessory to the State. This was a source of weakness, and it provides a reason for the stagnation of thought which came over the Eastern Church in contrast to the marvellous energy of the Church of Rome. It shows us, too, why the Church of Rome clung to its independence, striving to make its Popes the superiors of every earthly ruler.

Leo the Isaurian started the movement known as Iconoclasm, or prohibition of images in worship. Both in the East and West worship had by this time become very ornate, and the resources of art were used to the full in Christian churches. But in the East there was a strong feeling on the part of old-fashioned Christians against images, which, they felt, made Christian worship suspiciously like paganism. In the West this objection seems never to have been felt. Leo prohibited the use of images, and a long struggle ensued, the result of which was a compromise. The Eastern Church allows "eikons," or figures in relief, but not solid statuary. The images were defended on the ground that they were but symbols of Christ, or the Saints, and that the honour offered to them passed on to the beings they represented; which seems a reasonable defence, except that it is the same as that made by Dion Chrysostom in the second century for the worship of Zeus and Apollo.

Meanwhile in the West the Popes continually asserted their claims, and if possible increased them. That they should have power to curb lawless feudal princes in Germany and France was, as we have seen, almost a necessity. But they aimed at more than this. Nicholas I. interfered on behalf of Ignatius, Patriarch of Constantinople, who had been unjustly deposed from his office. He excommunicated Ignatius' successor, the learned Photius, who had been elevated from lay rank to the Patriarchate in six days. But the Eastern bishops were unmoved. They condemned the Pope at a Synod in 867 and even accused Rome of heresy. The breach thus caused was made definite two centuries later. The churches of the southern part of Italy had from the beginning been Greek, and subject not to Rome but to Constantinople. Leo IX., a vigorous Pope, wished to reform them on Roman lines. This led to a quarrel with Michael Cerularius, Patriarch of Constantinople. In 1054 Leo sent messengers with a letter excommunicating Michael and all who followed him. The letter was laid on the high altar of the Church of the Holy Wisdom. Thus East and West were separated. Whichever side was the more to blame God alone can tell; but assuredly the schism was a grievous harm to the Church.

The next two centuries were largely occupied by the Crusades, those unhappy attempts to make Christianity dominant by force of arms, in the Mohammedan manner. The Eastern Church took little or no part in them. Indeed, one so-called Crusade, by gross treachery, captured Constantinople itself, and established a Latin Empire and Church there for nearly sixty years, an indignity which the Greeks did not easily forget. In 1261 the Greek rulers regained the Empire, but with diminished strength. The Turks, the less cultivated inheritors of the old Saracen Empire, advanced through Asia Minor, crossed by Gallipoli into Europe and gradually surrounded the capital. Efforts were made to obtain help from the West and to reconcile the two divisions of the Church; but, although the Emperor and Patriarch might agree to the latter, the people were steadily opposed to submission to Rome, the price demanded for help. A last attempt at union was made on the very eve of the fall of the city. Messengers of Pope Nicolas V. were there with a letter demanding reconciliation, which the Greeks, in their extremity, had perforce to accept. But it was too late. Let me give the last picture in Dr. Kidd's words: "On the night of 28th-29th May, 1453, the last Mass was said in St. Sophia—Emperor and nobles, Patriarch and Cardinal, Greeks and Latins, all present—they made their last communion: for they knew that the assault was to be delivered at dawn. Then Constantine mounted his horse: and rode out to the defences. He perished sword in hand in the breach by the Gate of St. Romanus. 'God forbid,' cried the last Emperor of the Romans, 'that I should live an Emperor without the Empire! I will die with my city!'"

Thus Constantinople with its noble church passed to the infidel.

III

In the last section I drew attention to the splendid achievement of the Church of Rome in taming the barbarians of Western Europe—that is, our forefathers. It must not be supposed from this that the Eastern Church was idle. When Western Europe was in its "dark ages," and culture, humanity and religion were fighting for their very life, at Constantinople Roman Emperors ruled over a vast and prosperous empire. Let me quote Dr. Kidd's words again: "Wise administration was traditional with the Byzantine bureaucracy. It was the mark of a civilisation which distinguished the Empire from the barbarous kingdoms of the West. Trade throve under its protection; and sustained in prosperity a large middle-class, unknown in regions where there were only nobles and peasants."

Nor was the Church asleep. Bulgaria, it is true, was Christianised from Rome in the ninth century. But its King, Boris, gave his allegiance to Constantinople, which recognised a free and self-governing Bulgarian Church, a thing Rome would not do. The northern countries, Denmark, Scandinavia and Iceland, also owed their Christianity to Rome in this period. But the crowning achievement of the Eastern Church was the conversion of Russia. Just as England became a strong and united nation under William the Norman, so, nearly two centuries before, a Scandinavian adventurer named Rurik had begun the consolidation of Russia. Rurik's son Oleg made his capital at Kiev, and threatened Constantinople itself from the north. This has been called a " Norman Conquest of the East." Once communication had opened between Kiev and the Christian capital, missionaries became active, and there was soon a bishop at Kiev. In 957 Queen Olga of Russia, a widow, was baptised when on a state visit to Constantinople. She tried hard to win her young son Sviatoslav to her new faith. " My retinue would laugh at me," he replied. " If the Prince were once baptised," she said, " all his subjects would follow him."

This method of being converted *en bloc* with your Sovereign does not suit our ideas, although it has some practical advantages when you are dealing with people who are not easily able to judge the questions at issue. At any rate, it was the method often followed in old times, and in Russia Olga's words came true during the reign of Sviatoslav's son Vladimir. He was a remarkable person. He was called by Nestor the Chronicler " a second Solomon," because of the enormous number of his wives and concubines. But he was also a great conqueror, and apparently during his expeditions he watched to see what was the most suitable religion for his country. After trying the old heathenism, with human sacrifices, he examined and rejected Mohammedanism, Judaism, and the Roman Catholic faith. But when his messengers came to Constantinople they were amazed at the splendour and reverence of the worship in St. Sophia. They wrote to their master : " There is no such spectacle on the earth, nor one of such beauty; we cannot describe it; we only know that there God dwells in the midst of men." This caused a complete change in Vladimir. He married Anna, sister of the Emperor Basil II., and became a Christian, breaking down the idols he had formerly worshipped. He issued a proclamation that anyone who refused to be baptised with him, be he rich or poor, would fall into disgrace. And so a new nation was added to Christendom.

Let no one imagine, however, from this brief account that the conquest of Russia for Christ was an easy matter. The self-denying labours of many thousands of unknown men must have been necessary, over a period measured by centuries, before this vast land was covered and its simple people taught, even in a rudimentary way, the faith of the Church. This work was chiefly done by monks, just as was the conversion of Western Europe, including Britain. Only in the secluded life of monasteries could men in those days have opportunity to read and think, and by prayer to gather the spiritual energy needed for so immense a task. Dr. Frere says : " The monasteries were the chief evangelistic agencies. From the earliest days of Russia's conversion these outposts were being pushed forward, civilising and Christianising, across the great open spaces, over the interminable steppes, and even up to the cold sea in the inhospitable north. Where any less concentrated or less continuous agency would have been useless, they succeeded; setting up a warm centre of light in a wide and cold area of darkness, and gradually extending their influence till the district was won." Thus the bishops were always chosen from the monastic orders, among which alone was the necessary learning to be found. The ordi-

nary clergy, however, were allowed to marry. This rule is observed amongst almost all the Eastern Churches to this day,
although outside Russia it has a longer history and a somewhat
different origin.

It has often been noticed that Christianity has taken deep root
in all the lands west and north of its original home, but has little
to show in the lands far to the east. Yet in the beginning the
eastward spread was as marked as the westward. Great Churches
existed in Syria, Mesopotamia and Persia, and even the invasions
of Mohammedanism in the seventh century seem to have done
them little harm. Missionaries from these Churches pressed forward in a constant stream to India, Turkestan, Tibet and as far
as China. By the year 800 we hear of the Patriarch of Baghdad
consecrating a bishop for Tibet, and learning of the death of the
"Metropolitan of China." How far these Churches really
affected the life of Asia is doubtful; certainly not in the way that
the Western Church moulded Europe. But they were very
numerous, and cannot have been unimportant. Communication
with Europe was difficult and infrequent, and something of that
virility and eager activity which marks European Christianity
must have been lacking in Asia. But there are traces of bishoprics
from the Caspian Sea to China and from Siberia to India, and by
the thirteenth century their numbers amounted to many hundreds. An account is extant of one bishop, Rabban Sauma, who
set out from China in 1287 to visit Europe and negotiate an
alliance for his prince, Argoun Khan, with the object of retaking
Jerusalem from the Mohammedans. He was received at Constantinople and at Rome, where he was allowed not only to receive communion but also to celebrate his own Eucharist. "The
language is different," said the Romans, "but the rite is the
same." They did not realise, however, that these Far Eastern
Churches were Nestorian. The teaching of Nestorius, who became Patriarch of Constantinople in 428, was that the Word of
God united Himself with the man Jesus in a union that, although
close and inseparable, was not a union in essence. This seemed

to the Church to divide Christ into two persons, one human and one divine; and it was condemned on that account. But the Nestorians, when driven out of Syria, found refuge in Persia, and from them came all these Churches that we have spoken of. To this day, at Si-ngan-fu in China, there stands a monument which witnesses to the activity of these Nestorians.

Where, the reader may ask, have all these Churches vanished to? Not long after Sauma's visit to Europe, the great Tamerlane arose in Turkestan and started on his career of conquest over the whole of Central Asia. As a result, Christianity in those regions was all but destroyed, only a few remnants surviving. As in North Africa, the Church fell before Islam. It is a grievous story for Christians. But there is one survival of interest to members of the Church of England. Readers have probably heard of the Archbishop's Mission to the Assyrian Christians. These Assyrians are a relic of this ancient Christianity, and Archbishop Davidson befriended them. In gratitude they fought for England in the Great War. Since then they have suffered much from the Iraqians, but the surviving remnant are now being settled in Syria. Their Patriarchate has for several centuries been hereditary, passing from uncle to nephew. Only a few years ago the Patriarch, Issai Mar Shimun XXI., a young man of twenty-one, was studying at St. Augustine's College, Canterbury, as a ward of our Archbishop. This is but one example of the friendly relations which have grown up in recent years between the Church of England and the Eastern Churches.

IV.

The Eastern Church is divided from the Church of Rome, as we have seen, on the question of Papal supremacy, which the Easterns will not admit. But it has a number of other points of difference from the West taken in a wider sense, including the Church of England. These are both interesting and important in view of the widespread desire for reunion. The Orthodox Church, as its name implies, lays the greatest possible emphasis on right doctrine. This doctrine, it contends, was defined once and for all in the Nicene Creed, which was not completely formulated until the Council of Chalcedon in 451. But there are three Councils after Chalcedon, ending with the Second Council of Nicæa in 787, which are regarded as œcumenical—that is, of universal authority—by the Church. All the decisions of these Seven General Councils are accepted by the Orthodox Church. The basis of the faith is Holy Scripture; but this may not be interpreted by each person in his own way. The words of the Fathers, and the general tradition of the Church, must be taken into account.

Accordingly, the Orthodox Church rejects all " innovations," not because innovations must of necessity be wrong, but because they should not be adopted without the consent of the whole Church. The earliest of these was an addition to the creed itself, which we use to-day in common with Rome. The Creed of Chalcedon runs, " I believe in the Holy Ghost, the Lord and Giver of life, who proceedeth from the Father." In the sixth century a custom arose in Spain and Gaul to add the words " and the Son " (filioque). In 589 a Western Council at Toledo added this phrase to the creed. In spite of the protests of the East and the hesitation of Popes the phrase obtained a place in the creed and could not be dislodged.

The cause of the insertion of these words was that in the Gospel, although our Lord says that the Spirit " proceedeth from the Father," He also says, " If I depart, I will send Him unto you." There were practical and devotional reasons why it was good to insist that the Spirit of God is the Spirit of Christ; but the East was adamant on the impossibility of adding to a creed once accepted by an Œcumenical Council. The West was, and still is, regarded as heretical by the East on this account. But it does not follow that there is any fundamental difference of thought between the two. It has been suggested that " proceedeth from the Father through the Son " would express what both sides believe.

In the Orthodox Church that which we describe as Confirmation is administered immediately after Baptism. The priest obtains Holy Oil which has been prepared and blessed by the Bishop, and with this he anoints the baptised person, who then receives the communion, even though a child. The words spoken are, " The Seal of the Gift of the Holy Ghost, Amen." The baptism and the anointing, together with laying-on of hands, are regarded as parts of a single rite. This was the primitive custom, going back to times when most baptisms were of grown-up people. In those days, too, baptisms were not too numerous, and were reserved for special seasons when the bishop could be present. When infant baptism became the rule, the bishop delegated his authority for baptism to the local priest, keeping his connexion with the rite, however, by sending the consecrated oil.

In the West a different development occurred. The bishop retained the rite of Confirmation in his own hands, and consequently it had to be deferred until he could be present. It was administered to many at a time, and not to any under seven years of age. At the Reformation this usage was continued by the Church of England. But the anointing with oil, not being found in this connection in Scripture, was abandoned, and only the laying-on of hands retained. For the age of seven there was substituted the phrase " years of discretion," which has been variously interpreted. It is curious to notice that when, in the ninth century, the Pope objected to Photius, Patriarch of Constantinople, on the ground that he had been wrongly intruded into that See, Photius replied by accusing Rome of heresy, not only in the matter of the *filioque* clause in the creed, but also for insisting on the celibacy of the clergy and for confining Confirmation to bishops.

Those who have seen an Orthodox celebration of the Eucharist are struck with the difference of customs between East and West. Here, as in other matters, the Church of England follows Rome and the West, with which we are, both historically and by temperament, more closely connected than with the East. In Western churches the altar is open, but in the East the Eucharist is celebrated behind curtains. There is, it is true, with us a tendency to put up heavy screens which obscure the view of the altar, but these are simply a copy of monastic churches, where the monks naturally closed in a church for their own use, leaving the nave for visitors. The typical Western custom is seen at St. Paul's Cathedral or at the Roman Catholic Cathedral at Westminster. The Eastern custom is in strong contrast to this.

Another difference lies in the kind of bread used in the Eucharist. The Easterns use leavened bread, and strongly object to any other. Rome insists on unleavened bread, while in our own Church both uses are found. Two things seem clear; first, that the bread used by our Lord in the Institution was unleavened; and secondly, that for centuries the Church, in West and East alike, used nothing but leavened bread. Probably little thought was then given to the matter. But in later times it was found convenient in the West to use unleavened bread. The East, however, true to its custom of preserving things unchanged, uses the leavened bread still.

The Orthodox Churches have passed through evil days. Their history has been one of suffering, far more than ours has. When you suffer you cannot experiment; you simply hold on. They have been loyal to the faith as they have understood it, and as it has been handed down to them. Those who know them best assure us that they are by no means asleep, or unaware of the need for movement and adaptation in a changing world. Some think that to them may be given the task of converting Islam, at which up to the present the Western Church has conspicuously failed. Anyway, they have devotion to Christ, and they have love to their Christian brethren far beyond their own borders. And where love is, barriers and difficulties can never be insuperable.

PART II

THE FREE CHURCHES

CHAPTER I

CONGREGATIONALISTS

WHEN men have wished to reform what they considered to be abuses in the Church they have turned naturally to the New Testament to discover what the Church was like in the days of the Apostles. This is right and proper. But there are two warnings to bear in mind. One is that even if you could make to-day an exact copy of the primitive Church it would not serve for a world which is totally different from the world of the first century. The Church keeps her faith unchanged, but she must adapt her outward form to the needs of a changing world. To do otherwise would be like trying to return to the clothes which we wore when children.

The second warning is this. We must not read our own wishes into the New Testament. Some men have had a strong desire for a simple Church organisation. They have found what they wanted in the New Testament by the easy method of ignoring the many evidences of order and authority which it contains. Of this tendency Congregationalists seem to me to be an outstanding example.

Congregationalists originally called themselves Independents, a name which well describes their principles. For they maintain that any group of Christians may join together, make a covenant with one another and with Christ, and thus form a Church. This Church is independent and self-governing, acknowledging no obligations to other Churches, although it would preserve friendly relations with them. Contrary to the practice of the Baptists (who organise on the Congregational model), Congregationalists have always retained infant baptism; yet they claim that their adult membership is confined to strictly

Christian people. It is a Church of the saints, in contrast to the Church of England, which reckons all baptised persons to be members, although some are not very loyal ones. Each Congregational Church has the power to choose and ordain its own ministers, and it admits no rights of any external authority whatever, owning simply the lordship of Christ, as it understands Him. In recent times these principles have been modified of necessity; for they are clearly only applicable to small bodies of men struggling to exist in a hostile world. But Congregationalists would not, I think, repudiate them.

Each Church, thus independent in government, is also independent in creed. None may dictate to others. That is why Dr. Orchard remained a Congregationalist for so long, while teaching scarcely disguised Romanism. All he needed was the assent of his Church. Others, as a Congregational minister told me not long ago, may even doubt whether Jesus Christ ever existed. But this theoretical anarchy has worked out in practice to a fairly general uniformity, and nearly all Congregationalists have until recently taken the theology of John Calvin for granted as the self-evident interpretation of the Gospel. A national Church has always seemed to them wholly wrong; it contradicts the very notion of Independency. And it goes without saying that any association of the Church with the State is against Congregational principles. But practice has not always squared with theory; and where Congregationalism was dominant, as in the New England colonies between 1638 and 1727, the Churches enjoyed the support of the State, both in money and power.

In England, under stress of a common repression, Congregationalists and Presbyterians have often worked together, and still, I think, do; but their basic principles are poles asunder. The one is local, the other catholic, in outlook. It is true that Dr. Selbie, in his interesting book on *Congregationalism*, says that " from the first Congregationalists conceived of each individual Church as representing and being an outgrowth of the one Church." But this occurs as a footnote on page 179, and it shows how much could be written without such an important fact coming into the writer's consciousness.

Clearly in the New Testament organisation is somewhat fluid and rules of belief and practice are not yet fixed. But who can find there any "independent" Churches? The Council of Jerusalem spoke with authority, and not in a merely advisory capacity, when asked to decide on what terms Gentiles might enter the Church. Ordinations were conducted by ministers, such as the Apostles, who had power to do what they did. I think there would have been difficulty if one of St. Paul's Churches had claimed to act independently of him; and when he was no longer able to supervise them himself he appointed Timothy and Titus for that purpose.

For the beginnings of Congregationalism we must look to the reign of Elizabeth. Church services had been simplified and put into English, but episcopacy had been retained. Many people, however, wanted far more drastic changes. To them the Prayer Book, so beloved to-day, seemed sheer popery; and they said so. Some decided to wait, hoping in time to gain the ascendency and force their views on the rest of the Church. Others demanded changes at once, "without tarrying for any." Accordingly they became "Separatists," leaving the Church and forming societies on their own lines. A leader appeared in Robert Browne, who in fierce language denounced the existing form of Church government and exhorted his followers to refuse all "ungodly communion with wicked persons"—that is, those who were satisfied with the Prayer Book. Browne had a troubled career. After a time he conformed more or less to the established order, and was appointed schoolmaster at St. Olave's, Southwark. Later on he was ordained, but his churchmanship was never strong. Early Congregationalists were called Brownists after him; but, as was natural, they did not like the title. Browne's writings do, however, set forth clearly the Congregational position.

A number of Congregational ministers were put to death in Elizabeth's reign. Chief among them were Barrow, Greenwood and Penry, who were accused of treason because they denied the Queen's supremacy in matters of religion. This supremacy was the simple result of having a national Church; it did not mean that the Queen in person had power to determine Christian doctrine. But these men were adamant. " No prince, neither the whole world, neither the Church itself may make any laws for the Church other than Christ hath already left in His Word." They were no traitors, and their execution is a stain on our history; but they were hard men to deal with, since they claimed the right of deciding what Christ's laws were, and condemned all who disagreed with them.

The persecutions led many Congregationalists to settle in Holland, and afterwards, in 1620, to venture on the more famous journey in the *Mayflower* to America. Here they could put their system into operation without hindrance. In England they had a brief spell of power under Cromwell. The Long Parliament which opposed Charles I. and his Archbishop, Laud, had obtained the help of the Scots on the condition that when successful they should establish Presbyterianism in England. But Presbyterianism did not suit the ordinary Englishman, and still less did it suit Cromwell and his secretary, John Milton. These were men of marked individualistic temperament and, as is well known, it was Cromwell's army of Independents who secured the victory for Parliament. Cromwell soon tired of Presbyterian rule. He turned its supporters out of Parliament and established his own system, in which Independent ministers occupied a large proportion of the parishes of England. At the Restoration these men were ejected and the Church clergy restored.

For the next century Congregationalism suffered, as did other forms of Dissent, first from active persecution and then, after the Toleration Act of 1689, from minor political disabilities. It is lamentable to think that bishops should have supposed that the Church could gain by refusing common rights to Nonconformists. An interesting Congregational figure of this time is Isaac Watts, the hymn-writer, author of " O God, our help in ages past " and " When I survey the wondrous Cross." The revival under Wesley infused fresh life into all English religion, and Congregationalists were influenced by it, though they liked the Calvinist Whitefield better than Wesley.

In the nineteenth century Congregationalism has moved onwards, not hesitating to modify its old ways in order to secure greater effectiveness. The Congregational Union, formed in 1832, was an attempt to remedy the isolation and exaggerated independence of the " Churches." The London Missionary Society had been founded earlier, in 1795. It has the credit of sending out Livingstone, among other great men. But the chief innovation is the recent appointment of nine Moderators who, though their powers are carefully restricted, will doubtless come in time to fulfil the same function that bishops fulfil among us. Side by side with these external changes has gone the practical abandonment of Calvinist teaching.

If we look at the principles of Congregationalism, or study its early history too closely, it would seem hopeless ever to expect reunion between its adherents and ourselves. Yet things are not really hopeless, for thoughts are wider and sympathies warmer on both sides than they used to be. We can appreciate the individualism, the strong desire for freedom, shown by men like the Pilgrim Fathers, or by Milton, even when we think their aims might have been attained in better ways. Congregationalists, too, are learning the need for union, if not for authority, which the Catholic Church has discovered through centuries of experience. If we say that they are altering their principles, they may reply that even the Church is not quite the same to-day as it was in the seventeenth century.

CHAPTER II

PRESBYTERIANS

THERE were Presbyterians before John Calvin, says Dr. Moffatt. That may be so. But, historically, we must go back to John Calvin at Geneva in the years 1540 onwards for the origin of Presbyterianism. Calvin was a Frenchman, destined for the law, and possessing the clear, logical mind of his countrymen. When only twenty-six he published his *Institutes*, a work of immense ability, setting forth a theology and constitution for a Church in accord with the new reforming ideas. This book contained, in essence, the Presbyterian system.

Calvin maintained that the terms *bishop* and *presbyter* in the New Testament referred to one and the same order in the Church. *Presbyter* means elder and *episcopos* or *bishop* means overseer, and originally these were not distinct offices but different descriptions of one office. Hence Calvin objected to the bishops of the Church who ruled over presbyters and people alike. He wanted one order of ministers, all of whom should be essentially equal, though he recognised that for purposes of government it might be necessary to place some presbyters in a position of authority.

Besides the presbyters who are ministers, there are in Calvin's system others who are laymen. These are called " elders." They take part in the government of the Church and in administering discipline, but they do not preach or administer the Sacraments. They might be compared with our churchwardens, except that, being solemnly ordained to their office, the religious nature of their work is more strongly emphasised. Whatever may be the scriptural authority for them, or the lack of it, one cannot help seeing that here is a way in which laymen have been unmistakably reminded of their share in, and responsibility for, the spiritual work of the Church.

Calvin was a theologian and an organiser, not a fierce fighter like Luther. It was almost by a chance that he was enabled to work out his system at Geneva. The Genevans had gained the liberty of their city from the bishop and the Dukes of Savoy, who had formerly ruled it. Consequently, although not all the citizens were opposed to the old Church, they were forced into opposition because the bishop was allied with foreign enemies who threatened their freedom. A new religious system, independent of the bishop, had to be constructed; and Calvin, who passed through Geneva for a single night only, was pressed to stay and direct the reform. This he did, though not without many difficulties. For his system aimed at making Geneva a model city, in faith and in morals. Strict scrutiny was made of the citizens' characters, and offenders were handed over to the civil authorities for punishment. It was harsher than the Inquisition, so many felt. But Calvin and his fellow-enthusiasts had their way in the end.

The Calvinistic system allowed no toleration. Its methods of persecution were similar to those of the Church when that was in power. The best known instance is that of Servetus, a theologian of unorthodox views, who took refuge in Geneva and was apprehended and burnt at Calvin's instigation. It was a crime equal to any that can be laid at the door of the Inquisition. To-day the Genevans have erected a statue to Servetus, witnessing to their abhorrence of the deeds of those cruel times.

Presbyterianism has flourished best in Scotland. John Knox, a priest of reforming views, became a disciple of Calvin and returned to Scotland to put his principles into practice there. There was much opposition to the Church, partly because of the persecuting spirit displayed in the burning of George Wishart, and partly because the Church was closely connected with the French alliance. The Scots were now ready for independence and for friendliness with England rather than subservience to

France. Consequently the fight for freedom and the struggle for religious reform were intermingled, and the Church was forced into a reactionary position. When Mary Queen of Scots married the French Dauphin it seemed to patriotic Scotsmen that their country would become a vassal to France. This kindled widespread zeal for religious changes, and when Mary returned to Scotland she was forced to listen to Knox's preaching.

By English aid the French were driven out, but Mary's folly turned her people against her, and after 1560 the Presbyterian system was established in Scotland. Presbyteries, or synods of presbyters and lay elders, were instituted for Church government, and for a time superintendents took the place of bishops. Yet there was still a possibility of a settlement on reasonable lines, until Charles I., relying on his conviction of divine right, tried to force his will on the Scots. This brought them on to the Parliament side in the civil war, and for a brief space it seemed that Presbyterianism might be established in England as well as in Scotland. But Cromwell and Milton had other ideas. To them presbyter seemed but " old priest writ large." The Scots were repulsed to their own land, and Independency was established in England until the Restoration brought the old Church back again.

In Scotland the Presbyterian Church occupies the position which the Church of England has with us. That is to say, it succeeded to the buildings and possessions of the pre-Reformation Church. St. Giles' Cathedral, Edinburgh, so often pictured in the newspapers, is now a Presbyterian church. So is the parish church which the Royal Family attend when they are at Balmoral. But whereas we claim, and claim justly, that we have retained the essentials of the Catholic system, the Presbyterians gave up episcopacy for the reason stated above.

In doctrine, too, the Calvinistic system departed widely from Catholic tradition. Its central feature, that God is absolutely supreme and His will absolute, is indeed derived from St. Augustine. A corollary to this is that some men are destined by

God to eternal bliss and others to eternal woe, regardless of any efforts they themselves may make. In Catholic theology after St. Augustine's time this severe predestination theory had been considerably modified; but Calvin reintroduced it in all its harshness. In the *Westminster Confession*, which is the standard of Presbyterian doctrine, there are statements on this subject which modern Presbyterians, influenced by the humaner thoughts of our time and the better understanding of our Master's teaching, are anxious to alter.

It is contended that the Presbyterian system, in spite of its harshness, perhaps because of it, produced a brave and strong character which, in the Netherlands conspicuously, was able to withstand the tyranny of Spain. The Scots, too, have proved themselves a hardy and vigorous race. This love of freedom is a fine quality, and yet I doubt whether it has been less evident in England under the more genial influences of our Church. In Scotland it also produced violent internal dissensions, the history of the past two centuries being, according to a Presbyterian writer, " a perfect kaleidoscope of separating and reuniting sects." The bitterness and futility of these, together with the finer traits shown in them, may be seen in *The Little Minister* and other novels by Sir J. M. Barrie. On the other hand, the subtle cruelty which the system could inflict on sensitive and artistic souls is well portrayed in William Black's novel *A Daughter of Heth*.

The various divisions of Presbyterianism in Scotland are now ended, let us hope for good. That we in the Church of England have not suffered them must be largely due to the Episcopal system. The Scots think that we are bound, but we do not feel the fetters; and it is an undoubted fact that the Church of England contains men of wider divisions of opinion than any other body of Christians, and that she is in the forefront of the advance towards a more enlightened religion, carrying on the good traditions of the past and yet in touch with the knowledge and needs of the present. But there would seem to be no insuperable obstacle to our ultimate union with Presbyterians. Papacy and

" Prelacy," against which they fought, are not the same as a constitutional Episcopacy. And it is to be remembered that Presbyterians, at least those of Scotland, agree with us in regarding the ministry as an essential element in the Church, solemnly transmitted by the laying-on of hands, with a succession going back to apostolic times. They claim to possess this succession, though in a presbyteral and not episcopal form, and they do not admit that any company of men professing the same opinions can meet and form a true Church and elect a minister. This claim to catholicity is important. In Dr. Moffatt's book, *The Presbyterian Churches*, I do not remember seeing the word Protestant even mentioned, though " Catholic " occurs constantly. On the questions at issue scholars and divines must decide. Our business is to pray that, where so much of aim and principle seems common, means may one day be found for us to work in union and not in opposition.

CHAPTER III

BAPTISTS

EARLY in the sixteenth century, after the shock of Luther's challenge to the Papacy, there arose in Germany and Switzerland groups of people who felt that Luther had not gone nearly far enough, but that more radical changes were needed in the Church. These extremists were called by their opponents (both Catholics and Lutherans) Anabaptists, or people who baptised their converts over again. For they did not acknowledge the baptism of infants to be true baptism. In the New Testament, according to them, baptism was always administered to adults upon repentance and a confession of faith, and this "believer's baptism" they regarded as essential. As all their adherents would have been baptised in infancy in those days the practice did amount to re-baptism. In other matters also the Anabaptists departed no less widely from tradition. They were organised in small groups on the Congregational model, rejecting any association with the civil government. They favoured a communism of goods and were pacifists, refusing to bear arms. They recognised no authority but the New Testament, as they understood it. Some held these views in a moderate form, and were quiet and harmless folk. But others carried them to extremes, and combined with them prophecies of the speedy end of the world and the establishment of a kingdom of the saints. Such men were looked upon as a danger to social life, and when in 1543 a crowd of fanatical Anabaptists, abandoning their pacifism, captured the town of Münster, and established there a horrible régime of Communism and polygamy, opinion turned more strongly than ever against Anabaptism. The Münster revolt was suppressed, its leaders were tortured and killed, and the moderate Anabaptists elsewhere were severely persecuted. Every Reformed Confession of Faith contains a denunciation of the Anabaptists. In Art. 37 of our Thirty-nine Articles we are told that " It is lawful for Christian men, at the commandment of the Magistrate, to wear weapons and serve in the wars." And Art. 38 adds that " The Riches and Goods of Christians are not common, as touching the right, title and possession of the same, as certain Anabaptists do falsely boast."

Now the English Baptists disclaim any connexion with the Anabaptists, and no one would suggest that they have ever practised or countenanced any political excesses. Quite the reverse. But their central tenet, that which their name signifies, is " believer's baptism." For a good while they were called Anabaptists in England, but not unnaturally they disliked the name, and now for long they have stood among us as a distinct denomination under the title of Baptists.

It is often conceded by churchmen that on the point of New Testament practice the Baptists are right, and that the baptism of infants, as a universal Church custom, is a late development dating from the fifth century. Even if this were so, the practice might well be defended by those who believe that the Holy Spirit was in the Church, guiding and sustaining it, through all its history and not only in the sixteenth century. But when Professor Wheeler Robinson says that " no one has the right to argue that the baptism of the New Testament is less than the immersion of intelligent persons," he goes too far. The matter is by no means so certain. Clearly, when a new faith is being proclaimed, it must first be addressed to adults; and, speaking generally, infants are not likely to be included until a generation or two has passed. That is what happens in the mission field to-day. But when three thousand were baptised on the Day of Pentecost, were they all grown-ups? Is it not possible that children might be included? And were they all immersed? There are difficulties here, when one comes to think the matter out, which should make us pause before accepting the Baptist position as self-evident.

Much is made of St. Paul's attitude to baptism, and his teaching about the necessity of faith. Yet in the Church of Corinth there was a custom of allowing people to be baptised on behalf of their dead friends. Whatever may have been the wisdom of this practice, or the reverse, it shows an extraordinary anxiety that everyone should be baptised. Is it likely that men who attached so high an importance to baptism would have left their children unbaptised? Or, when the goaler of the prison in Philippi was baptised in the middle of the night, " he, and all his, immediately," was there an age limit under which exclusion from the baptismal ceremony was necessary because the very young could not understand " the Word of the Lord "? I cannot bring myself to think so.

What is certain is this, that there did grow up in the third and fourth centuries a fear of being baptised, because it was supposed that sins committed after baptism could scarcely, if at all, be forgiven. There are frequent examples of men, such as Constantine the Great and St. Augustine, whose baptism was deferred for this reason. Later on, when the stress of persecution was over, Christians could think of God as more merciful and less harshly severe, and they brought babes freely to the font to be sealed there with the mark of the Cross, leaving them to learn afterwards how wonderful was the blessing which God had given them. The Church justified this by appealing to the example of the women who "brought their young children to Christ that He should touch them." In spite of all the logic of the Baptists, I feel that the Church's instinct was right.

But to return to history. The first English Baptists were John Smyth and Thomas Helwys, the latter of whom founded the first Baptist Church in London in 1611-12. This was composed of " general " Baptists, who believed that Christ died for all men. But between 1630 and 1640 there was formed in London the first " particular " Baptist Church, whose members were Calvinists, believing that Christ died only for the elect. The "particular" Baptists have always been the preponderant body, and scarcely any "general" Baptists now exist; but, as with Congregationalists, the doctrine of Calvin has been largely abandoned by modern Baptists, so that the word "particular" has lost much of its meaning. Except for their insistence on "believer's baptism," Baptists agree in principle with Congregationalists. Each local "church" is independent, and any church member may preach, administer the Sacraments or perform any church function whatever without ordination. In practice, of course, these principles have to be modified. There is a Baptist Union, a ministry carefully trained and set apart, and even "General Superintendents."

The Baptists have never enjoyed great worldly prestige, such as the Independents had under Cromwell; nor, to do them justice, have they ever sought it. William Allen, the Baptist officer who took part in the "Windsor Castle Prayer Meeting," when the Army leaders resolved to bring the King to trial if ever they had the power, was afterwards a severe critic of Cromwell, whom he called a "ghost from the grave" of the Stuarts. But the most striking figure in Baptist history is John Bunyan. The tinker of Elstow was not bred in the Baptist community. He came to it, and was always but loosely connected with it. He is a universal voice, speaking of experiences which touch the heart of every man. But the Baptists have the glory of giving him a home, and we of the Church the sorrow of remembering that when so mighty a prophet arises, too often we cannot find room for him. In days when men's minds are full of plans for material prosperity, often with nothing more satisfying than ease and comfort as their goal, and when the eternal issues are often kept deliberately out of sight, the pilgrim may still turn for courage and refreshment to the dream of this seventeenth-century workman, which, as a modern writer has well said, "continues strangely to haunt the world, and bids fair to outlast many other dreams and schemes proclaimed in their day as the final wisdom."

Another remarkable man was William Carey, the shoemaker

who became a missionary to India and a linguist and translator of amazing energy. Missionary enthusiasm did not run high in 1786. When Carey hinted that the obligation to teach all the nations was still binding on Christians, he was told by the presiding minister to sit down. " When God pleases to convert the heathen, He'll do it without consulting you or me." We have all moved a little since those days! Within living memory the name that stands out most conspicuously is that of C. H. Spurgeon, whose preaching at the Metropolitan Tabernacle drew multitudes for many years. As I write these words, I have looked once again into my volume of Spurgeon's sermons. In spite of a marked narrowness of outlook, and a very real unlovableness in some respects—legacies of Calvinism—one cannot but be impressed by the simple eloquence of these addresses, their insight into human life, and their devotion to Christ. God fulfils His plan in unexpected ways.

Baptists, like the rest of us, are passing through times of change to-day. Curiously enough, a question among them is whether baptism should be counted a necessity for Church membership. There are " open " Churches which do not insist upon it. It would indeed be strange if those who began by holding fast to this one distinctive practice should end by neglecting baptism altogether.

The gap between Baptists and the Church is, as will be seen, a wide one. On paper it seems unbridgeable at the moment. But as the position of religion in the world becomes more critical God may show ways that are not visible on our horizon yet.

CHAPTER IV

QUAKERS

DR. INGE, in his book, *The Platonic Tradition in English Religious Thought*, says that "the Quakers, of all Christian bodies, have remained nearest to the teaching and example of Christ." I am not sure whether this means that the Quaker system is the one which our Lord would approve before all others if He were with us in the flesh to-day, or that the Quakers are more Christlike in conduct than other Christians. Whatever may be the interpretation, the quotation is prefixed by Dr. Rufus M. Jones to his book on *The Faith and Practice of the Quakers*, and we may conclude that he accepts it, not without a certain satisfaction. For myself I doubt the wisdom of either making or accepting such sweeping assertions. Many readers of this book will have, I suppose, a quiet confidence that our Church of England system is as near as any other to the mind of Christ. If we knew a better we should change over to it. But we have much to learn from those who differ from us, and in fact we are continually learning. As for conduct, there are saints in every Christian community; and although the Quakers have produced a distinct type of saintliness, it would be a daring thing to say that our Lord would value that above any other. John Bunyan had vigorous contests with the Quakers, and who will say that he was inferior to his opponents in the saintly life? Yet the fighting, struggling, sin-laden Bunyan was the very antithesis of the silent, pacifist, God-inspired Quaker. Christianity is a big religion, and has room for many varieties of character.

The antithesis just mentioned will give a good idea of the religious position of the Quakers. Luther was the father of all

Protestants of the kind to whom sin and the individual need for redemption were the outstanding facts of human life. He took his doctrine from St. Augustine, who had strongly emphasised the depravity of our nature. But there were other men in Europe as dissatisfied as Luther was with the ways of the Church, but looking for reform in quite a different direction. They called themselves " Seekers." They abandoned all outward forms— ministry, sacraments, creeds, liturgy—and waited in silence until the Holy Spirit moved them to speak. Their belief was that each human soul might be a channel through which God could make known His will. They rejected all systems of theology which seemed to deny this, and particularly the dogmas of Calvin, which taught that most men were irredeemably separated from God. They formed small communities in which they lived a simple brotherly life, the sort of thing that is possible for a few picked men detached from the main currents of the world, but which becomes far more difficult when you try to save the world from within it.

Such a man in England was George Fox, the founder of Quakerism. Born in 1624, he was a quiet, meditative youth, and became strongly dissatisfied with the Calvinism prevalent around him. He left home and travelled about the country seeking someone who could bring him light; for he was convinced that the Church in general was wandering in darkness. Gradually, by meditating on the Bible, he felt the light of God dawning within him. He had little education and no knowledge of history. But from the Bible he obtained flashes of understanding which made him certain that the guidance of the Spirit was open to all. Everything else contained in the Bible, the history of the Church, for instance, with its officers and sacraments and theology, he passed over, concentrating attention on this one truth that had become plain to him.

Changed by this experience from a weak youth to a courageous man, Fox began to spread his ideas. It is clear to us that the positive part of his teaching was not really opposed to the practice of the Church, which in every century had nourished mystical souls like his own. There is need, of course, to take care, and to test the spirits, whether they be of God or the mere imaginings of the human mind. But Fox, like many another reformer, wanted to cast down as well as to build up. He attacked the clergy, the " steeple-houses," all rites and ceremonies, together with music and art. In his desire for a simple life he would not even raise his hat; and he used " thee " and " thou " instead of " you," because these words appeared in Scripture. In short, he exchanged one set of forms for another. Such extravagances weaken his title to our admiration, though much in his character is noble and praiseworthy.

Around Fox there grew up a body of people calling themselves the " Children of the Light." Soon this gave way to the term " Society of Friends." The word " Quaker " was at first applied to them in derision. Many of the ranting sects of those days actually did quake during their meetings, and doubtless Fox's followers often did the same. They suffered much persecution, not only from the government in England, but also from the Puritans who were in power in America. Nevertheless they increased in number, their converts including Margaret Fell of Swarthmoor Hall, and later on William Penn, who obtained from Charles II. a charter to found Pennsylvania.

The Quakers lay stress on the mystical experience of Christ through the Spirit, which they rightly contend should be shared by every believer. To provide an atmosphere for this experience their meetings begin in silence. Everything around is bare, the object being to have nothing which may distract the attention from inward contemplation. The Church acts on the opposite principle, that colour, sound and form are means through which God may be apprehended, and not barriers to shut Him out. In a Quaker meeting each speaks or prays only when he is " moved " to do so, and Quakers testify that this form of worship, both in its silence and its utterances, is productive of real spiritual refreshment.

Wonder is often felt that Quakers can accept the New Testament and yet reject the sacraments, for which we have the express commands of our Lord and the clear practice of the apostolic Church. Fox regarded sacraments as " man-made " ordinances. Obsessed with the notion that forms and symbols must be a hindrance to the Spirit, he claimed to be able to obtain the grace which the sacraments convey without using the appointed means. Quakers still make this claim. They are more at home with St. John's Gospel than with the others. Their meditations dwell on life, light, love and truth, those profound spiritual conceptions which permeate this Gospel. But they forget that St. John's Gospel was written for people for whom Baptism and the Eucharist were the crucial events in the Christian life. The Christians of Ephesus would indeed have been surprised to learn that the life and the love were in conflict with the sacramental rite; for they found the one in the other, as we do to-day.

Latterly, however, the more learned Quakers have sought another way out of this difficulty. They deny that our Lord instituted sacraments at all. The command, " Do this in remembrance of me," appears in St. Luke only, and not in St. Matthew or St. Mark. Certain scholars have concluded from this that St. Luke borrowed the phrase from St. Paul's account in 1 Corinthians xi., and that St. Paul obtained it in some of his mystical experiences and not from any authentic tradition of the words of our Lord. Frankly, I do not understand how scholars who are churchmen can take this view and be easy about it. If St. Paul really invented the Eucharist, as a Christian rite, it is hard to see on what grounds we could pay it the reverence that we do. I cannot argue the matter at length here (although I should be prepared to do so at some other time, for I regard it as important), but my conviction is that we have ample reason for believing that our Lord did enjoin this rite, in order that it might be the means of fellowship between Himself and His disciples, and of communicating to them His own life throughout the ages. It is quite wrong to suppose, as so many do, that our Lord would be, as it were, more spiritual if He took no measures to establish a society on earth and to frame the general principles on which that society should develop. I believe that He showed wisdom and foresight in this as in all His teaching.

The Quakers have always been pacifists, and are everywhere respected as such, though not all of us would agree with them. Drawn chiefly from the middle classes, they have prospered in business and have in recent years shown themselves model employers, as the names of Cadbury and Rowntree testify. The Adult School movement is largely their creation. Though they did not fight, they were active and generous in tending wounded and stricken folk in the war and afterwards. Having shed the queer garb and speech of a " peculiar people," they now mix freely in ordinary life. No people are more lovable. In spirit and outlook we differ scarcely at all, but how there can be union between those whose whole religious life centres round the sacrament of love and those who reject it altogether is a thing I cannot see.

CHAPTER V

UNITARIANS

THE Unitarians trace their descent from some of the Cromwellian ministers who were ejected from their livings in 1662 because they would not agree to the Act of Uniformity. Much sympathy is expended on these men by modern writers, and no one can deny them the credit of holding strong opinions and being ready to suffer for them. But it is often forgotten that there is even more sympathy due to the Anglican clergy who were ejected under Cromwell. They were forbidden to teach or to hold services or use the Prayer Book, and many who disobeyed this harsh law were imprisoned and barbarously treated. Those who survived were restored to their parishes in 1662.

The period of severe persecution of Nonconformists did not last long. As soon as the Toleration Act was passed, in 1689, chapels sprang up all over England. There were 750 of them at the beginning of the eighteenth century. These chapels were called Presbyterian, but this seems to have been only a broad name to distinguish them from the Church, for most of them were founded upon what are called " Open Trusts "—that is, Trusts in which no specific doctrines were laid down. No doubt it was taken for granted that the chapels would continue to stand for the current Calvinism, but the fact that they were not tied to particular doctrines made it easier for some of them to develop, as they did later on, into Unitarianism.

Early in the eighteenth century there was considerable discussion in England about the doctrine of the Trinity. This doctrine was not completely formulated and finally established in the Church until the Council of Chalcedon in 451. Before this time much thinking had to be done and many erroneous ideas rejected.

Once the doctrine was accepted, however, it proved a guiding and steadying influence in the Church, which has been of incalculable value. But when men left the Church and cut themselves adrift from its accumulated experience they had to start afresh to gather their faith from the Bible. Consequently ancient heresies tended to revive.

The first form of Unitarianism was therefore a doctrine akin to the heresy of Arius. He was a presbyter of Alexandria early in the fourth century, and, being imbued with Greek ideas of the divine, he supposed Christ to be not the Eternal Word begotten of the Father, but an intermediate being hovering between earth and heaven. He thought that the Greeks, who were accustomed to worship various grades of deities, would accept Christ in this form as the highest and first created being. This not only robbed Christ of His true divinity, but also of His true humanity, although Arius did not see that. The doctrine could be plausibly supported by certain New Testament passages (*e.g.*, 1 Cor. xv. 28 and Col. i. 15), but to arrive at the true implications of these passages it was necessary to take into account the experience of the Church during her three centuries of worship. English Unitarians of the eighteenth century, rejecting the Church tradition and reasoning from the Bible as they then understood it, came to conclusions very much like those of Arius. It is important to note, however, that modern Unitarianism has altogether abandoned the Arian position; and Dr. Martineau went so far as to say that, in the controversy that ended at Nicæa, his sympathies were more with St. Athanasius than with Arius.

In 1719 there was a dispute at Salter's Hall in Exeter, on the question whether the doctrine of the Trinity should be regarded as a necessity for dissenting congregations, or whether the Bible should be interpreted with complete freedom. The result was a split, in consequence of which some chapels became known as Non-subscribing. From these arose the modern Unitarian chapels. They were still called Presbyterian, but they moved more and more in a Unitarian direction during the eighteenth

century. Prominent in this movement were Joseph Priestley and
Theophilus Lindsey. Priestley was a scientist, and his chief title
to fame is the discovery of oxygen. But he was a theologian
also, and his works run into many volumes. He became Unitarian minister of Mill Hill Chapel in Leeds in 1767, and later
on of the New Meeting Society in Birmingham. Owing to the
sympathy he expressed for the French Revolution, which he regarded as a great blow struck for liberty, his house and chapel
were burned down by the mob in Birmingham, and his books
and scientific instruments destroyed. It was a deplorable act,
for Priestley had many saintly characteristics, and he was fighting a battle for freedom of opinion which has benefited others
besides Unitarians.

Lindsey was a Churchman, Vicar of Catterick in Yorkshire.
He took part in a movement to free the clergy from subscription
to the Creeds and Articles. At that time it was said that there
was far more Arianism in the Church than among the Dissenters.
Lindsey and his friends presented the " Feathers Petition " (so
called from a tavern in the Strand) to Parliament in 1772.
When it was rejected he resigned his living and opened a chapel
at Essex Street, Strand. This " Essex Chapel " was from the first
definitely Unitarian, and it became very popular among people
of unorthodox religious views.

These early Unitarians were moved partly by a desire to stress
the Unity of God, and partly by a dislike of the ordinary doctrine of the Atonement. They reacted much more against a
harsh Calvinism, which we should repudiate as warmly as they,
than against the true doctrines of the Church, which they had
scarcely an opportunity of understanding aright. They accepted
the Bible as inspired, but they denied that it taught what churchpeople and Dissenters alike found in it. Their peculiar characteristics were a passion for reason and common-sense, a desire for
clear-cut, intelligible doctrines, and an aversion from the mysterious. It was only in 1813 that they were made legally free to hold
their opinions, and in 1884 that, after a struggle, their chapels,

which under the Open Trusts had gradually changed from Presbyterianism to Unitarianism, were secured to them by law. After this the character of Unitarianism has altered considerably. Unitarians were among the first to welcome the critical study of the Bible. They regard this as establishing their contention that Jesus was no more than a man and that the stories of His birth and resurrection are unhistorical. They pay Him the deepest veneration, and believe His life to be the expression of the ideal for man, but they do not worship Him. Nevertheless they try to get beyond the dry, matter-of-fact rationalism of their predecessors, and to infuse devotion and mystical fervour into their appeal.

In the nineteenth century Dr. Martineau stands out among English Unitarians. He was a theologian of great intellectual power, and was respected far beyond the limits of Unitarianism. To him the basic authority for religion was no longer the Bible, nor the Church, but the reason and conscience of man. Yet he gave Unitarians a sense of the value of the past, which is not, as they were inclined to think, one continuous series of errors. Towards the end of his life Martineau, while still retaining the Unitarian beliefs, learned to appreciate better the creeds and worship of the Church. Modern Unitarians are even more anxious to make their religion a fellowship, with roots in the past, and not merely a philosophy.

But when all is said, the bias of Unitarianism is distinctly intellectual. This has rendered it the least popular of all forms of Dissent. But, on another side, it has resulted in much educational activity. Many of the Academies of the seventeenth and eighteenth centuries were directed by Unitarians. In 1783 the Warrington Academy was removed to Manchester and became the Manchester New College. After a period at York it again migrated to Oxford, where it is now well known as Manchester College.

Churchmen and Dissenters alike are wont to regard Unitarians as a class apart, far removed from the common faith.

Some would even deny them the name of Christian. We need not, however, exaggerate differences, some of which may be more in the manner of expressing our faith in words than in the living faith by which our souls are sustained. We owe much to Unitarians. How many are aware that " Nearer, my God, to Thee " was written by a Unitarian? Recently Dr. L. P. Jacks was asked to preach in Liverpool Cathedral, and a great controversy ensued. Concerning this it is not my business to judge, but I have read Dr. Jacks' sermons in a little book entitled *Elemental Religion* (Williams and Norgate). They contain many moving and inspiring words, which give me at least the hope that in spite of our acute differences there exists a genuine unity of heart which may one day, with God's blessing, widen into a unity of worship.

CHAPTER VI

METHODISTS

THE eighteenth century is often called a time of Church deadness. Hunting and drinking parsons, locked churches, neglect of the sacraments, alienation of the poor and the like are thought to be its characteristic features. But the description of the country parson in Goldsmith's *Deserted Village* tells a different story, which must not be overlooked.

> " A man was he, to all the country dear,
> And passing rich on forty pounds a year.
>
> .   .   .   .   .
>
> At Church, with meek and unaffected grace,
> His looks adorned the venerable place.
> Truth from his lips prevailed with double sway,
> And fools, who came to scoff, remained to pray."

There must have been many such parsons in England then. And if worldliness was prevalent, as it undoubtedly was, it is also with us to-day, though it presents a more respectable exterior.

The truth is that the beginnings of the Industrial Revolution caught the Church, as they caught the State, unawares. Populations grew up with great rapidity, needing new methods of evangelisation because the existing parochial system could not cope with them. It was this problem that John Wesley set himself to meet. The son of Samuel Wesley, Rector of Epworth in Lincolnshire, and Susannah his wife, he was brought up in an atmosphere of evangelical piety and sent to Oxford. Here he did well, and was elected a Fellow of Lincoln College in 1726. With his brother Charles he joined a group of men who met for study and prayer and bound themselves by rules of fasting and regular Communion.

They were called "The Holy Club," or the "Methodists," because they lived by rule.

From Oxford he went in 1735, after ordination, to Georgia, a new American colony, as a missionary. Wesley was an individualist, intolerant alike of authority in those above him and of independence in those below. His dictatorial methods soon caused trouble in Georgia, and an unfortunate love affair put an end to his work there. He returned to England sad and dispirited.

When in this condition he met in London Peter Böhler, a Moravian, through whose spiritual counsel he underwent a conversion. At a religious meeting in Aldersgate Street one of those present was reading Luther's preface to the *Epistle to the Romans*. "About a quarter to nine," says Wesley, "when he was describing the change which God works in the heart through faith in Christ, I felt my heart strangely warmed. I felt I did trust in Christ, Christ alone for salvation; and an assurance was given that he had taken away my sins."

After this experience Wesley started on his campaign of revival. The clergy were suspicious of his new enthusiasm, expressed in terms foreign to their sober ways of thought and worship. It is not quite fair to say that the churches were closed against him. He acted everywhere on his own initiative, acknowledging no superior and regarding the world as his parish. A similar revivalist to-day would not find it easy to preach in Methodist churches, especially those in well-to-do neighbourhoods. Looking backward, we can see that the bishops and clergy were unduly afraid of Wesley, yet we must admit that the disturbances which accompanied his preaching gave them some reason for their fears.

At this point Wesley was joined by Whitefield, a fellow-student of his Oxford days and an ordained priest of the Church. Whitefield preached in the open air outside Bristol and other large cities, and after some hesitation Wesley followed his example. Large crowds attended these preachings, which sometimes lasted from early morning to late evening. We are told of miners down whose blackened cheeks the tears ran in streaks of white. The fervid oratory of Whitefield and the more restrained addresses of Wesley were alike helped by the hymns of Charles Wesley. Some of these have now become the common property of Christians, as a glance at the index of any hymn-book will show. We can well understand that they brought into the lives of simple men, pressed down by poverty and sin, an exultation and a hope unknown before.

Wesley was a born organiser. Whitefield's impressive preaching produced little result, for his people were, as he put it, " a rope of sand." Wesley never preached without forming a society of the converted and binding them to simple rules of life. Thus arose the Class Meeting, and the Society which knit the classes together. The needs of the work forced him also to employ lay preachers. It was this organisation which ultimately caused the separation from the Church of England. For Wesley, in creating his Society, had made it dependent entirely upon himself and without any attachments to the Church. It is true that he wished his people to go to communion in their parish churches. It is true also that sometimes they were refused communion. But many of the Methodists were by temperament and upbringing out of sympathy with the Church of England, and in their view they had in the Society all that was required for a Church—ministry, order and worship. Wesley fought against secession, but he was illogical, as his brother Charles saw. Certainly the bishops and clergy were none too sympathetic; but Wesley himself was responsible for the breach by his own impatience of control and by the wonderfully effective organisation he had brought into being.

In 1784, when the Methodist Societies in America were increasing, Wesley took the novel step of appointing Dr. Coke as " Superintendent " and of ordaining two preachers, Vasey and Whatcoat, as " elders." Dr. Coke was not called " bishop," but he acted as such, and from him the Methodist Episcopal Church of America takes its beginning. Coke was a priest of the Church of England, and had just as much, or as little, right to consecrate Wesley as Wesley had to consecrate him, but Wesley regarded himself as raised up by God for a special purpose, which gave him privileges and responsibilities denied to others.

Though Whitefield and Wesley always remained friends, they differed totally in theology. Whitefield was a Calvinist, whereas Wesley preached that God's grace was freely offered to all without exception. Whitefield's name is familiar in London through the "Tabernacle" in Tottenham Court Road, as is Wesley's by Wesley's Chapel in the City Road near by. But Whitefield found a friend in Selina, Countess of Huntingdon, who favoured his type of theology and endeavoured, through his ministry, to revive religion among her aristocratic friends. She established proprietary chapels in Bath, Cheltenham, Brighton and other fashionable centres, some of which continue to exist to-day as chapels of "Lady Huntingdon's Connexion."

Wesley died in 1791. Whatever we may think of his judgment, his life was amazing enough. "For fifty-two years he preached, visited his societies, entered prisons, galloped along the highways of England, the programme varying but little, and yet he never became stale." Immediately after his death Methodism detached itself from such connexion as it had had with the Church of England and formed itself into a separate body, ordaining its own ministers and directing its members to receive the sacraments at their hands. Wesley's evangelistic work was a personal thing, as such work always is; and the Methodist Church became like any other dissenting body, a society that ministered to the needs of those who liked its peculiar type of religion and worship. Methodists have this disadvantage, however, that they do not stand for any distinctive point of teaching or order, as Baptists and Congregationalists do.

It is a curious thing that the Methodists, who left the Church because their irregular ways were not welcomed, should have driven from their own body men who differed from them on comparatively unimportant points. First Kilham, who wanted laymen in the annual conference, was expelled in 1796 and formed the Methodist New Connexion. There followed Hugh Bourne, who revived the enthusiastic open-air meetings and was suspected by the ordinary Methodist who worshipped in a chapel, as Wesley had been suspected by churchpeople. Thence came the Primitive Methodists. The Bible Christians arose in Devon from similar causes, and the United Methodist Free Churches gave the laity rights which the older-fashioned Methodists were not willing to concede.

Fortunately, this story of secession is now ancient history. After many years of effort the Methodists of Great Britain now form one body. The union has been a great achievement for which others besides Methodists may thank God. May it be a prelude to the day when they will return to the old Church of our country, which, be the fault ours or theirs, they ought certainly never to have left.

CHAPTER VII

THE "CATHOLIC APOSTOLIC" CHURCH

I MUST explain at the outset that this "Catholic Apostolic" Church has nothing whatever to do with the Roman Catholic or any other part of the historic Catholic Church. It is the name adopted by a society that came into existence about a hundred years ago. Its members have been commonly called Irvingites, because the society had its origin in the work of Edward Irving; but they resent this designation, and so I have given them their official name.

The "Catholic Apostolic" people are now a small and declining body. Edward Irving died on December 7, 1834, and his followers and successors have never been numerous. As, however, the "Church" is a somewhat bizarre society, it is right to give here a few words of appreciation of Irving. Edward Miller, in his *History of Irvingism,* says : "His was a truly noble nature. There was nothing base, or petty, or weak in his composition, if we may say with entire justice as we certainly may with partial truth, that even his errors were strong." And Thomas Carlyle, a life-long friend, though poles asunder from Irving in religious views, writes thus in his *Essays* : "One who knew him well, and may with good cause love him, has said, ' But for Irving I had never known what the communion of man with man means. His was the freest, brotherliest, bravest human soul mine ever came in contact with; I call him, on the whole, the best man I have ever, after trial enough, found in this world, or ever hope to find.' "

Irving died of consumption, intensified by his labours, at the age of 42. In a day of small men, it is heartening to read words like those I have just quoted.

Irving's birth was at Annan, in Dumfries, on August 4th,

1792. He became a schoolmaster and then entered the Presbyterian ministry. As assistant to the great Thomas Chalmers, at Glasgow, he was overshadowed, but when he came to London to be minister of the Caledonian Church in Hatton Garden he obtained a great reputation almost immediately. It is said that Canning was taken by Sir James Mackintosh to hear Irving preach, and was so impressed that he referred to the sermon shortly afterwards in the House of Commons as the most eloquent address he had ever heard. The result was that all London flocked to Hatton Garden on Sundays.

The substance of Irving's preaching was the approaching coming of Christ and the Millennium—that is, Christ's reign of a thousand years upon the earth. Irving, like others, got this doctrine chiefly from the books of Daniel and Revelation. In days when the true method of interpreting these books was unknown there was always danger that ardent souls, reading without the aid of the traditional wisdom of the Church, should be led into wild and fantastic speculations. The time, too, was one of unrest. Men still remembered the terrible French Revolution and the meteoric career of Napoleon. Machines were being invented and life seemed to be going onward to unknown changes. The fact was, as we know but men of Irving's day did not, that a new age was opening which would bring great blessings to men; for the Victorian age is not to be despised. But many interpreted the signs differently, and thought that the end of all things was at hand. Such people found in Irving one who answered their needs.

About this time conferences were being held at Albury Park in Surrey by a group of ministers, both Church and Dissenting, and laymen, on the same subject. The president was Henry Drummond, the banker, and Irving was invited to attend. These conferences concluded that the coming of Christ was near, and that to avert the dreadful judgments which would accompany it a special outpouring of the Spirit was necessary and to be expected.

Consequently there arose in Irving's congregation " prophets " —that is, persons who spoke with " tongues," in a confused and unintelligible way. They brought great disorder into the worship, as their predecessors had done at Corinth in the first century. But Irving was no St. Paul, capable of dealing sympathetically and yet firmly with these outbursts. He had preached that the Spirit was to come, and lo! the event had happened, and he sincerely regarded the utterances of the " prophets " as inspired.

This phenomenon of " prophecy " bears a strong resemblance also to Montanism, a wave of uncontrolled enthusiasm which disturbed the Church at the end of the second century. Montanus asserted that he was the mouthpiece of the Holy Spirit, and he was aided by two prophetesses, Prisca and Maximilla. They proclaimed that the new dispensation of the Spirit was come, and that Christ was about to return to earth. The very spot where He would descend was determined, a mountain in Phrygia, and to this place great numbers of their converts repaired. But the Church had learned by this time to see the Holy Spirit's operation in the orderly development of its life and the spread of its Gospel, and it refused to be drawn away by these extravagances.

Irving's " prophets " (he was never one himself) soon designated certain men as " apostles." These became eventually twelve in number, and they were chosen, not for any observable fitness to play the majestic part assigned to them, but solely on the prophetic utterances. Both Irving and his people, however, accepted them without question. The rule of his congregation was transferred to these men, and he himself, whose preaching had given rise to the whole movement, was ordained an " angel," or bishop, by them, for without prophetic authority he was allowed to do nothing.

At this point Irving falls into the background. He had previously been deposed from the Presbyterian ministry, and after less than two years of insignificance in the new community he died. But the " Catholic Apostolic " Church was now in being, with Apostles, Prophets, Angels or Bishops, and Elders and Deacons, all of whom were laymen at work in the world. They conceived their mission as follows: The Apostles were to take into the world a message that the Kingdom was near. They were to deliver it to the Pope, to Kings, Archbishops, and all rulers of the Church. As the original Twelve accompanied our Lord at His first coming, so this second Twelve were to be heralds of His second coming. Together they make up the twenty-four of Rev. iv. 4.

The apostles who travelled about Europe made no great impression on the world. But from observation of Christians in other lands they gained a knowledge, often concealed from the stay-at-home Englishman, of how Church worship has been conducted throughout the centuries. So they adopted for their own services a liturgy, compiled largely from Eastern sources, and an elaborate ceremonial, with vestments, incense, holy water and the like. Seven churches were established in London, and all, I believe, still exist, the best known being that which meets in the stately Gothic building in Gordon Square.

But the whole *raison d'être* of the community was the approaching coming of Christ. This was confidently expected to happen during the lifetime of the Twelve; but one by one these passed away, the last dying some fifty years ago. Now that its early faith has been so completely disproved, it is hard to see what the " Catholic Apostolic " Church stands for. It seems that its members are guilty of no heretical teaching, and it is clear that they recognise the true Catholic Church as existing far beyond their own borders, and so are free from the arrogance which often characterises small sects. Why they still maintain a separate existence and do not return to the Church which they profess to believe in, I cannot tell.

Certain it is that while the true Catholic Church must welcome the wide outlook of the " Catholic Apostolic " people, and respect their strong desire for the coming of Christ's Kingdom, she must look for that Kingdom not as a final catastrophe, the date of which is to be puzzled out, but as the reign of the Spirit in men's hearts. This is largely within our own power; nothing but man's unbelief and sin hinders the work of Christ on earth. When that work will be accomplished and the present dispensation brought to its close, we do not know. " Of that day or that hour knoweth no one, not even the angels in heaven, neither the Son, but the Father."

CHAPTER VIII

THE SALVATION ARMY

THE Salvation Army, like the Methodist movement, is the creation of one man. John Wesley and William Booth had many qualities in common, but what particularly distinguishes them both is a passion for the conversion of men, a marked unconventionality in method, and a genius for organisation. Booth himself was converted at the age of fifteen, when he decided that " God should have all there was of William Booth." He joined the Wesleyans, and became a local preacher and minister, until he found in 1861 that Methodist ways were too strait for him. Thenceforward he travelled about England conducting evangelistic services where opportunity offered. In all this he was helped by his young wife, a woman of fine character and remarkable courage, who stood by him with faith and devotion when times were difficult and the future far from clear.

In 1865 the Booths found themselves in East London. They saw focussed there, so Bramwell Booth tells us, " all the problems which arose out of a reckless and godless population, largely untouched by any civilising or Christianising influence, and presenting a very Niagara of poverty and vice." The sight led William Booth to dedicate his life to work among the poorest and most degraded. He said to his wife : " Oh, Kate, I have found my destiny! These are the people for whose salvation I have been longing all these years."

That there was in the second half of the nineteenth century much squalor and degradation in the poorer parts of London and other great cities is undeniable. These were the days when those who were able to profit by the Industrial Revolution could pursue their way almost unchecked, when slums were built and sweated labour was rife, while education and the social services had not kept pace with the increase of wealth and population. But we need not exaggerate the evils. Salvation Army literature, which is all written in a panegyrical vein, gives the impression that wherever there is poverty there is also vice and crime. This is not true. Nor can it be wholly true that the Church was without any effect on the lowest strata of the people or indifferent to their condition. Miss Friederichs tells us that though the outcasts came freely again and again to William Booth's Christian Mission they were not wanted in the churches. When such a " ragged, uncouth, ill-mannered creature . . . slouched into the church, where it was an unpardonable sin against good breeding to come ungloved and in work-a-day garb, then in not a few cases the excellently well-mannered Christian would move out of the heathen's way with unmistakable signs of disapproval, and his wife would hold her perfumed handkerchief to her face to avoid the danger of contamination." This is mere journalistic rhetoric. It is fairly safe to slander the dead, who cannot answer; but I refuse to believe that there was not a good deal going on in the East End parishes of a more tender and compassionate sort than that.

Nevertheless the Church system, with its solemn worship on traditional lines, is not suited to deal with the social outcast; at least, not in the first instance. Booth, like Wesley, was performing a notable Christian service when he addressed his appeal to the very lowest—to drunkards, gamblers and thieves. His first intention was to hand over his converts to the Church and other Christian bodies, but when he found them simply relapsing into their old condition, because they could not find a suitable spiritual home, he decided to create an organisation to receive them. For that nobody can blame him. The pity is that the new organisation was so framed that once a man had entered it he was for ever cut off from the Church and the sacraments. Wilson Carlile's Church Army, which was being formed at the same time, shows a better way. Carlile dealt with the outcast by methods even more unconventional than those of Booth. But he established a link by which the convert could make himself spiritually at home in the Church and be sustained by the sacraments. The two bodies, outwardly similar, are poles asunder.

As the Christian Mission grew its converts were employed in preaching to others, the workman to his fellow-workman, even the converted gambler and drunkard to their former associates. It was in 1877 that its name was changed to the Salvation Army. The new title was due to a sudden inspiration, but it suited its purpose so well that it became at once a permanent designation. The title " General " had been given to Mr. Booth before that, but as an abbreviation of " General Superintendent " and with no military meaning. When the organisation became known as an Army, however, other military titles were taken for its officers as they became necessary.

From the beginning the system of the Salvation Army has been autocratic, more autocratic than the Papacy, which in many ways it strongly resembles. General Booth felt himself called by God to direct and control the Army, and to exact unquestioning obedience from all under him. He was also sole trustee for all the Army's property. In the early days he claimed that this power was necessary in order to act swiftly, but it will be obvious that when the Army spread, as it has spread to every part of the world, there was considerable danger in concentrating so much authority in one man's hand. The Salvation Army, by its very principles, disallows any criticism of its methods or organisation. All officers are subordinate to the General, and have no redress in case of unfair treatment. Such a system must crush out all individuality, and, indeed, is meant to do so. But, like all dictatorships, it possesses a certain machine-like efficiency.

When General Booth died, he appointed his son Bramwell Booth to succeed him; and when his death drew near, only a few years ago, it became clear that he intended to keep the generalship in the Booth family. According to the Army's constitution it seemed that he had power to do this; but not unnaturally opposition arose, and a new leader, General Higgins, was appointed by a council of the higher officials of the Army. After a short period of service in this capacity, General Higgins retired in 1934, and the leadership then reverted to the Booth family.

In 1890 was launched the "Darkest England" scheme. General Booth appealed for funds to start farm training for unemployed men at Hadleigh in Suffolk, and to assist men to emigrate. The idea was not new, for Wilson Carlile had opened a Labour Home in the previous year, and had already formed plans for the wide extension of this social work. But the Salvation Army's well advertised scheme attracted much attention and secured large public subscriptions. To-day, besides Labour Homes, Shelters and an Emigration Agency, the Salvation Army runs its own Bank and Insurance Society.

The religious work of the Army has but one aim—conversion. Its dogmatic basis is a somewhat old-fashioned orthodoxy, in which the fear of hell still occupies a prominent place. But the Army does not engage in theological discussions; it is content with "soul-saving," which it endeavours to follow up with a life of rigid simplicity and often of great hardship. The worlds of thought, art and culture, which the Church links up with religion and strives to claim for Christ, are of little interest to the Salvationist.

The main defect of the Army, from a Christian point of view, is its neglect of the sacraments. To disregard the command, "Do this in remembrance of Me," was defensible in days when the Army aimed at being a feeder for the Church, but now that it acts as a fully equipped Church, and tries by every means to retain its members and increase their number, the neglect is harder to understand.

The belief is often held that the Salvation Army deals with those whom no other Church can touch. This, however, is not true. The Church Army works among all levels of our people, down to the lowest, and the Church in the poorest parishes is continually engaged in the work of reclaiming the flotsam and jetsam of humanity, although we do not advertise the fact. As national social services increase, the " Niagara of poverty and vice " which first melted the heart of William Booth will be reduced in volume; and already there are signs that the Salvation Army, as a religious body, is becoming as respectable as the rest of us. Every year, in the Self-Denial week or weeks, large sums are provided by an appreciative people for the Salvation Army. Much of this, one supposes, is devoted to social work; but some must be used for the religious organisation, with its large halls, Sunday Schools, Scouts, Guides and other activities, whose members come not from the criminal classes, but from just the same sort of people who are served by the church and the chapel.

PART III

VARIOUS SECTS AND DOCTRINES

CHAPTER I

BRITISH-ISRAELISM

IT is often supposed that when a man forsakes what we may call orthodox religion he becomes more critical of evidence and harder to convince. But experience shows the very opposite of this; for in numberless cases such men fall victims to the first superstition they meet, and believe the most astounding things on evidence that ought not to convince a child. Now superstition is religion without truth. If you take the elements of religion, such as reverence, imagination, worship, morality and the like, and set them adrift in life without truth to guide and control, you have an influence which may degrade rather than uplift, as history abundantly proves.

We should expect, then, that in the present neglect of religion superstition would abound. And indeed it does. British-Israelism is but one example out of many. But it is a peculiarly harmful one, and since some Churchpeople are puzzled by it, a word of explanation and warning may be helpful.

British-Israelites begin by drawing a sharp distinction between Israelites and Jews. Jews were inhabitants of Judah, and the ancestors of present-day Jews. It is obvious, from features alone, that these are a different race from Saxons or Celts; and so they stand in the way of British-Israel theory. Consequently the whole Jewish race, as known to us, is ruled out of any active share in the divine plan, which is, so we are told, that God's promises in the Bible are made to Israel only and not to Judah. There is, of course, no ground for separating the Hebrew race into these two distinct peoples; it is one race and always was. Logically, we may add, this theory would exclude Jesus Christ Himself, for He sprang from Judah (Heb. vii. 14); but British-Israelites are not logical.

In what way, however, can Israel, or the ten northern tribes, inherit God's promises, since they were led away captive into Assyria when Samaria was taken, about 721 b.c., after which they disappear from history?

This is the puzzle which the British-Israelite professes to solve. These captives, he tells us, did not remain in Assyria, nor were they gradually mingled with the heathen there, as is generally believed. They grew into a powerful people and migrated westwards, becoming in turn the Scythians, Goths, Saxons and Angles. Thus they arrived at last in England. It is claimed that we are descendants and the heirs (not in a spiritual sense, as St. Paul taught, but in a carnal, literal and national sense) of the divine promises.

The British-Israelite then remembers that we are a composite people, including Celt as well as Saxon. Indeed our name, Britons, is not Saxon at all. So the Celts must be brought in. This is done by introducing as sober history an obscure Irish legend which says that Jeremiah the prophet came to Ireland accompanied by an Egyptian lady who married an Irish chief. All you have to do is to change the Egyptian lady into the daughter of Zedekiah, the last king of Judah, and you not only bring the Irish into the supposed divine plan, but connect the Hebrew monarchy with Ireland. It is then easy—for the British-Israelites—to trace the descent of the English monarchy from Ireland.

English kings are thus direct descendants of the ancient kings of Judah. And, we are gravely told, is not one of our Prince of Wales' names David? But William the Conqueror is a difficulty. This is solved by making the " Joseph tribe " separate from the others in their westward trek and " reappear in history " in the year 800 as the Normans.

I need scarcely say that not a single one of these assertions has any foundation in history. They are mere figments of an unbridled imagination. But presented in dogmatic form, with a bewildering complexity of details, and an appearance of scholarship, they can and do deceive many who are unable to compare them with the facts.

It is further asserted that Jeremiah brought with him the stone on which Jacob slept, and that this was afterwards removed to Scotland and then to England, and is actually our Coronation Stone. No proof is even attempted of this absurd claim.

The object of all this is to show that Great Britain and the Empire, together with the United States, is God's chosen nation. All others, whether Christian or not, are without the covenant. In a few years' time—1934, to be precise (this prediction was made in 1932)—is coming "the final drama of this age," in which God's people (*i.e.*, the British Empire and the U.S.A.) will be arrayed in warfare against the rest of the world. Then will be the battle of Armageddon, in comparison with which the Great War of 1914-1918 will be "a mere breeze." God's people will be victorious, and His enemies (*i.e.*, French, Germans, Italians, Russians, etc.) will be "put down."

I shrink from reproducing this blasphemy; but the quotations are necessary. They will be found in *The National Message*, issued by the British-Israel World Federation.

Fantastic "proofs" are given to support the connexion of Britain with Israel, based on verbal assonances between Hebrew words, not as they actually are in Hebrew, but as they read in our Authorised Version. Saxons are "Isaac's sons"; Danes are the tribe of Dan; Scots and Scythians derive their name from *scoth*, the Hebrew for booths or tabernacles. But Isaac in Hebrew bears no resemblance to Saxon; and *scoth* should be *sukkoth*, a very different sounding word. Even more foolish is the statement that we have clearly possessed the "ships of Tarshish" promised to Israel, because our sailors are called Jack Tars. Such "proofs," which can be manufactured *ad infinitum*, are the ravings of minds steeped in abysmal ignorance.

Latterly the Great Pyramid of Egypt has been pressed into the service of this theory. A divine revelation is supposed to be made through the measurements of the Pyramid. But why the

Egyptians, who are certainly not Israelites, should have been the recipients and exponents of a revelation I cannot tell; any more than why the Saxons who remained in Germany should not be Israelites while those who came to England are.

It is hard to be patient with this nonsense, and one would dismiss it with a smile were it not that there are people among us who are attracted by it. And the matter has a serious side. A man who for some time attended my own church left us because we prayed for peace when, according to him, God had foretold war within the next few years. A hundred fanatics of this type would constitute a public danger.

The best cure for superstition is a patient study of the Scriptures, with the aid of modern books and commentaries, which the Church of to-day can supply in abundance.

CHAPTER II

"GREAT PYRAMID FUNDAMENTALS"

THE theory widely advertised under this title is akin to British-Israelism. Both are attempts to glorify the British Empire and the United States at the expense of other nations, and both appeal to a perverted patriotism. But whereas British-Israelism relies on the Old Testament, the "Great Pyramid" theory has chosen a fresh authority. British-Israelites, too, form societies and work through local branches. But the "Great Pyramid" theory rests mainly on the shoulders of one man, Mr. David Davidson, who addresses the world through full-page advertisements in *The Times* and other newspapers.

It may be asked, "What has the Great Pyramid to do with Christianity?" It has no more to do with it than has Stonehenge or the Great Wall of China, either of which would serve equally well as a basis for fanciful theories, if once you let the imagination run riot, free from the control of reason.

Here, briefly, are the facts. The Great Pyramid was built about 4000 B.C. by Khufu, sometimes called Cheops, a king of Egypt. Egyptian religion was greatly concerned with the after life. Men desired that their bodies should be preserved in a secure dwelling surrounded by objects which had been useful to them here. It was thought that so the soul would be enabled to live a life in the other world corresponding to its condition in this. As the soul's welfare was supposed to be dependent upon the state of the dead body, elaborate precautions were taken to prevent the tomb from being desecrated. That is why tombs of kings and nobles were made so huge and strong. The Great Pyramid is the largest and most wonderful tomb ever made. It well repays study. But to say that it has any meaning beyond this is to make assertions without evidence. It is sheer romancing.

The "Great Pyramid" theorists maintain that the Pyramid was so built as to predict future history. The measurements of its passages, walls, ceilings, etc., when correctly interpreted, are said to give us a record of every year of the period from the Autumn Equinox of 4000 B.C. to the same season of 2000 A.D. This date represents the coming of the Messianic Kingdom; in other words, the end of the present world.

This amazing claim is derided by all competent Egyptian scholars, one of whom calls it "lamentable nonsense." Their authority will be sufficient for most people, and I need only repeat here what I have said in a previous chapter, that prophets of the end appear in every age. Any strange or mysterious thing, such as the books of Daniel or Revelation, or now the Great Pyramid, gives them material enough to work upon. By juggling with figures they profess to foretell the future. When their predictions are falsified, as they always are, they are quite unashamed, and simply push their dates a little further forward. They have a show of learning which impresses many, and their books and pamphlets find a ready sale among the unthinking, who sometimes leave the faith which has come down to us from the days of the Apostles to lose themselves in these dreams and fables.

But let us consider the proofs which these theorists offer in support of their doctrine. First, Mr. Davidson disposes of all previous workers in the same fields. Their opinions—*i.e.*, their prophecies of what was soon to happen, but actually did not happen—were "ill-grounded and fallacious.'" The truth only emerged a few years ago, with Mr. Davidson.

Next, it is seriously maintained that the Great Pyramid was built by a white people, the Building race who are ancestors of the Anglo-Saxons. But Herodotus, the Greek historian who visited Egypt, says that the Pyramid was built by the forced labour of 100,000 men, and took twenty years to build. These men were Egyptians, as was the king who ruled them. The inscriptions in the Pyramid are also Egyptian. It is pure fancy to imagine anything different.

Then we are told that these builders worked to measures based upon an inch which is nearly identical with our inch. Egyptologists have rightly replied that the inch was unknown to Egyptians, who worked by cubits. Still less, I may add, is it possible that this inch was derived from a division of the earth's polar axis into 500 million parts. The people of 4000 B.C. would not have known that the earth had a polar axis, for they would have supposed it to be flat. Mr. Davidson admits, indeed, that Egyptologists are right in saying that the Egyptians did not use the inch. He attributes the use of it to the white " Building race," but these, as I have said, are a mythical people.

Lastly, Mr. Davidson makes much of what he calls the Theme of Displacement. According to him, the builders of the Pyramid made a mistake in their building, and this mistake is an allegory pointing to the faulty construction of the universe. Mr. Davidson means, apparently, that the builders did not construct the Pyramid as he thinks they should have done. I have not had the privilege of examining the Pyramid; but I should suppose that it was built according to plan, and that if we do not understand the reason for every detail, it is our knowledge that is at fault. But to take the details of an ancient building and imagine that they could possibly throw any light on God's method of creation is to lose all touch with reality.

I say, God's method of creation; but according to this theory God did not create the universe at all. Mr. Davidson re-hashes the old Gnostic idea that the material world is the work of inferior powers—" Cosmic builders," he calls them—and not of God. It is their error, or the imperfection of their material, which has caused the evil of the world. This is a dangerous heresy. The Bible says that God made the world, and pronounced it very good. Be the difficulties ever so great, Christians must hold fast the Bible teaching on this vital point.

The writings of theorists like Mr. Davidson appear so learned in their style that men unacquainted with the subject feel there must be something in them. But there is no limit to the absurdities into which men can be led. Every doctrine must be tested. And all the tests which intelligent men can frame show that this Pyramid teaching is but the baseless fabric of a dream.

Nevertheless it has a warning for us. These longings for the end of things, and hopes of God's miraculous intervention, are born of despair, which is not Christian. It is wrong to exaggerate the difficulties of to-day. There are successes as well as failures to record. Life is far easier, happier and kindlier for the mass of people than it was in past ages. Signs are not wanting that we are moving forward to a better world, where life will be more abundant, and much suffering, hitherto regarded as inevitable, abolished for ever. The Christian should not spend his time in contemplating wars and convulsions, but in working for peace. The Spirit of God is in the world to-day, speaking in the hearts of the living, and not through the tombs of the dead. The future is not irrevocably decreed; it lies largely in our hands. Let us thank God and take courage.

CHAPTER III

CHRISTIAN SCIENCE

LONDONERS, at least, are familiar with the ornate and costly structures which have arisen in their midst, bearing the modest but optimistic superscriptions, First, Second, Third and so on, Church of Christ Scientist.

The title is peculiar. Does "Scientist" mean scientific? Christian Science has no connexion with science as ordinarily understood. But the phrase has a high sound, and is probably meant to be impressive, without having any clearly defined significance.

But whatever we may think of the title the fact remains that we have here a new religion, born in our own time, complete with Founder, Sacred Writings, Organisation and Creed. How long it will last no one can say; but it certainly has *begun*, and nothing on a similar scale and with like pretensions has happened since the time of Mohammed. One can hardly call it a heresy, for its connexion with Christianity, which it contradicts on most essential points, is but slight.

Mrs. Eddy, the founder, was born in 1821. She was thrice married; first, to George Washington Glover, by whom her son of the same name was born. Glover died within a year, and another husband, Daniel Patterson, came along. The little son was sent away, and his mother never saw him for thirty years. Patterson, however, left his wife, and later on, when she was fifty-six, she married Gilbert Eddy, from whom she took the name by which she is known.

In youth she was frail and excitable, suffering from attacks of depression and hysteria. This continued till she was forty, when she met Phineas P. Quimby, a specialist in mind cures. Quimby had discovered the immense value of suggestion in the healing of disease. He used his knowledge to help the poor and sick, with little personal reward. Quimby had a sense of humour, saying that people sent for him and the undertaker at the same time, and the first who arrived got the case. His success was remarkable, and he made voluminous notes of his method so that others might practise it when he was gone. He believed, too, that this was the method used by Jesus Christ in His works of healing.

Mrs. Eddy came to Quimby a weak and emaciated woman. He gave her new life, and for some time she was extravagantly grateful to him. Then, starting on a business of her own, as a trainer of mind healers, she found it convenient to repudiate Quimby, and to assert that the knowledge was her own discovery.

Quimby was not merely a healer. He held a doctrine, too. He believed that health was natural to man, and that disease is due to a wrong condition of the mind. The mind influences the body and is superior to it. Up to a point this is sensible enough, and far preferable to a morbid dwelling upon suffering as if it were the chief thing in life and the most obvious expression of the " will of God." But much pain and suffering is the result of accident, over which the mind can exercise no control whatever. Quimby, and Mrs. Eddy after him, denied evil any reality at all, shutting their eyes to facts.

Thus did Mrs. Eddy, developing Quimby (for although she owed much to him she added much of her own), launch out into a sea of metaphysics in which she was ill-adapted to keep afloat. There is no objective world; only subjective ideas exist. All that we think to be the external world is due to the human mind, which itself is unreal, " carnal " or " mortal mind " she called it. It only deludes us. She denied that food preserved life; denied even that babies need be washed! No one could take such a philosophy seriously, and certainly Mrs. Eddy never attempted to live by it.

Her book, *Science and Health*, was first published in 1875.

It has undergone many changes since, to make it more suitable to the tastes of a critical public. The earlier editions are now very rare, most copies having been destroyed by the Christian Science organisation. Yet even in its present form, as any reader can obtain it from a library, it is an amazing book; not for its literary or philosophical qualities, but for sheer muddle and inconsequence. " There is no reason," says Mr. H. A. L. Fisher, " why the first chapter should not be the last, or the last the first. There is generally no reason why one sentence should follow and not precede another." And the wearisome length of it! " It would not have been thought possible," to quote Mr. Fisher again, " to expend so many words upon a theme which St. Paul would have made intelligible in a chapter or Voltaire in a page."

The teaching of the book is embodied in the three following axioms :

> " God is all in all;
> God is good, good is mind;
> God spirit being all, nothing is matter."

Mrs. Eddy observes that these propositions are proved to be true because they can be equally well understood when read backwards! This illustrates the mentality of those to whom the Christian Science campaign is addressed.

Many people, thousands of years before Mrs. Eddy was born, have believed that God is all in all. That doctrine is called Pantheism, and it reduces evil to a semblance. (The Christian doctrine is that God *shall be* all in all, a very different thing.) Others have gone further and believed that mind or spirit is everything and matter an illusion. You can hold that doctrine if you like, but you ought to hold it consistently and not make exceptions when it suits you. A friend of mine who lost an arm was told by a Christian Scientist that she still possessed the arm. So far so good. But if the loss of an illusory arm makes no difference, why should the loss of food or money make any difference either? Mrs. Eddy met this by saying that while men held false beliefs about the reality of matter it was necessary to use these things. But she herself, who knew the truth, should surely have known better? Yet her meals were carefully served, and she had an acute sense of the usefulness of money; for she amassed a large fortune, and took scrupulous pains to see that the unreal lucre was securely invested.

In spite of God being " all in all," there was, for Mrs. Eddy, much evil (error, she called it) in the world, illusory, but potent. Whenever she was ill (and she suffered all her life) she attributed it to the evil thoughts of persons whom she supposed to be her enemies. It was " Malicious Animal Magnetism," or M.A.M. A guard of defenders constantly accompanied her to ward off the attacks of M.A.M. Psychologists can give adequate reasons to account for such fears, quite different from these crude beliefs in bewitching influences, which though common among savages are now abandoned by most civilised men.

The transition from a " Metaphysical College," for the training of students in mind healing, to a " church " was probably not foreseen. But it proved a great success. Aided by press boostings in the customary American fashion, and reports of miraculous cures, the new religion attracted many adherents. *Science and Health*, which had at first been published only with great difficulty, now sold by thousands, and most of Mrs. Eddy's fortune came from the profits on this work.

It may be wondered why a religion with so shady a beginning should now appeal widely, as clearly it does. The reason is that it expresses, though with many perversions and exaggerations, a truth which Christians have often failed to realise—namely, that since God is love, He wishes His children to be healthy and happy. Joined to this is the fact, well known now, that a right mental and spiritual condition can work wonders on a sick body. A gloomy view of religion, with undue stress on our sins and weaknesses, is not the same as the triumphant attitude of St. Paul—" I can do all things through Christ which strengtheneth me." Jesus Christ came to take away men's burdens, not to add to them; and the Church to-day is recognising this more and more.

But to close one's eyes, as Christian Scientists do, to the pain and misery of the world, is cruel as well as foolish. It ignores the Cross. And, to say the truth, the Cross has no place in Christian Science. It is a religion for the comfortable only. It has had no martyrs, nor will have. You can easily go to folk in secure and pleasant homes and tell them that their little suffering are unreal; but the Church must deal also with the poor, the oppressed and the hungry. While she does that she need have no fear about the future, even if Christian Science conquered all New York.

For a man to give up the Faith for Christian Science is an act of moral cowardice. It means retiring from the fight with pain and evil into a dream world. Our Master never did that. He went into the real world, and so far from denying the reality of pain and evil, He bore them to the uttermost. This is the touchstone by which true Christianity must ever be gauged.

CHAPTER IV

SPIRITUALISM

I USE the term " Spiritualism " because it is widely accepted, and I do not wish to confuse the minds of any who may read this chapter. But I use it under protest, for the term is an inaccurate one. " Spiritualism " really means the doctrine of spiritual things —*i.e.*, of truth, beauty and goodness in all their manifestations. The true name for the doctrines concerning spirits should be Spiritism, and this is the title of the article on the subject in Hastings' *Encyclopædia of Religion and Ethics*, by Dr. F. C. S. Schiller.

Spiritualism in this sense is almost as old as humanity. It is found among the most primitive peoples, who have their wizards and medicine-men who claim to be able to communicate with departed spirits when such communication is desired. The instance best known to us is that recorded in 1 Samuel xxviii., when Saul, depressed by the host of Philistines arrayed against him, endeavours to get advice from the departed Samuel. He goes by night (these manifestations always happen in the dark) to Endor to visit a woman with a familiar spirit, or, in modern language, a medium with a spirit " control." She is able, or pretends to be able, to " bring up " Samuel—that is, to give him a certain temporary materiality so that he becomes visible to her and can hear and answer questions. The rest of the story is well known.

This practice of dabbling in the affairs of the other world has generally been regarded with aversion, and often prohibited by rulers with the support of public opinion. Saul himself, we are told, prohibited it until the last dark days when troubles were closing in upon him and his reason was failing. Isaiah speaks strongly against it (viii. 19), and it is forbidden in Deut. xviii. 10-12 and Lev. xx. 27. Isaiah's witness is interesting, for he tells us that the wizards used to " chirp " and " mutter," and in another place (xxix. 4) that they spoke as if " out of the ground." The Greeks called these necromancers *engastrimuthoi* (" speakers out of the belly," or ventriloquists), since they used this kind of speech to impersonate the spirits whom they were supposed to bring up from the world below the earth.

So far we are dealing with a phenomenon of primitive life, which tends to die out as rational knowledge advances and healthy religion takes the place of superstition. The Church from the beginning set her face steadily against it, and the general Christian belief of early times was that the communications, if genuine, were with the devil and his followers. But in order to satisfy the natural and proper desire of men for union with their departed friends, the Church taught the doctrine of the Communion of Saints, that our loved ones in Christ are near us, that they do not forget us, nor ought we to forget them, but that through prayer, and especially in the Eucharist, we may be with them in spirit, though we see them no longer.

In recent times light has been thrown on the multitude of obscure beliefs and practices connected with necromancy, or communication with the dead. The science of psychology has made us familiar with the subconscious, that deep well of mind-stuff from which such queer things bubble up at times. Telepathy and second sight appear to be established as facts, though their workings are not understood. Some people have a double personality, not in the limited sense in which this is true of us all, but in an extremely marked degree; so that when they change from one character to another, often quite different, they give the impression of being under the influence of a spirit which has entered in and taken possession of them. The medium of to-day, who answers to the ancient necromancer or witch, is a person of highly neurotic temperament, easily susceptible to states of trance or hysteria, in which rational control is abandoned and the subconscious asserts itself without guidance or restraint.

9

Nevertheless, modern science, in spite of advances in psychological knowledge, has not devoted the attention it should have done to the various phenomena of Spiritualism. The result is that these have been left, for the most part, to be exploited by persons who use them as a business, and who cannot therefore be expected to maintain the critical and dispassionate attitude of a scientific man towards them. This indeed is understating the case; for, as everyone knows, the path of Spiritualism is strewn with instances of deliberate fraud. Not that all mediums are fraudulent, nor even that any of them necessarily sets out with the intention of deceiving. But when the experiment fails, as it often must, there is great temptation to resort to trickery in order not to disappoint the inquirers. And precautions suggested by sceptical minds are resented as imputations upon the medium's honesty.

No one can be certain, therefore, of the precise value of the phenomena observed at spiritualistic séances. They may be due to telepathy or to some other curious workings of the human mind not yet understood, or they may sometimes be genuine communications from the spirit world. But from what sort of spirits —good, evil or merely freakish—is another question. Science must eventually decide.

The Church is interested in every branch of science and will gladly accept its results when these are fully proved. But she is not directly concerned with science, even on such a subject as human survival. Christians have their own faith in the after-life, based on grounds which the heart knows to be sufficient, and fortified by the message of her Lord's resurrection, a fact amply confirmed by nineteen centuries of Christian experience, in which His living presence has never yet failed them, nor fails to-day. To exchange this faith for " sight," when the sight is of shadowy apparitions in a darkened room, is a thing we do not wish to do. And while we should encourage and support any scientific investigations of the phenomena in question, we should strongly discourage all amateur dealings with them; for not only may amateurs easily be deceived—the gullibility of untrained minds has no limit, as the charlatan is well aware—but there are perils to body and mind, perils leading in extreme cases to insanity or complete moral breakdown, which beset the unwary. These are not simply orthodox bogies, but the reasoned warnings of spiritualists like Sir Oliver Lodge and Sir William Barrett.

Within the last fifty years or so, and increasingly since the war, Spiritualism has made a bid for popular favour as a new religion. In the present confusion of thought any pseudo-religious system, however wild or extravagant, has a chance of success if only it addresses itself to some tender spot in human nature—e.g., patriotism in the case of British-Israelism, removal of suffering in the case of Christian Science, and love for the departed in the case of Spiritualism—and is advocated with sufficient confidence. In fact, Spiritualism contains not a single one of the elements of religion. But when we are broken-hearted at the loss of dear ones it seems at the moment that communication with them is our deepest need, and we clutch at anything which promises to satisfy it, regardless of the loss in other directions. We must admit, too, with sadness, that the Church of England has been somewhat cold in her references to the departed. Not all of us could stand at the grave of a beloved friend, and still less of a husband or wife, and sincerely thank God for removing him or her from " the miseries of this sinful world." Heresies and sects always enter in at points where the Church has failed to do justice to her real teaching, which properly understood can answer every human need.

The pretensions of Spiritualism are amazing. It can communicate with anyone, from Moses to the last soul that has left this world. The " controls " who effect these communications, and who must apparently be possessed of superhuman (or should it be super-psychical?) knowledge, are quaint creatures with odd names such as Moonshine or Redfeather (Red Indians) and Feda, an illiterate coloured girl. They give us no spiritual knowledge at all, but content themselves with solving puzzles—e.g., saying where something is hidden, or making trivial remarks such as that the departed one likes his mother's new dress. When their condition is asked, they reply in general terms, saying that they are happy or that their friends must not worry.

If such communications were repeated ten thousand times, and even if they were authenticated, they would afford no materials for a religion, least of all for Christianity. For the first need of religion is God, and of Him the " spirits " give us no news worth recording. The next world will be a bare place indeed if it does not bring us a little nearer to God, so that He, now seen by us " through a glass darkly," shall become more real, more awful, more inescapable. Following this nearer vision will surely be a shame and deep penitence at our unworthiness in the presence of the All Holy. Of this the " spirits " seem to be utterly unconscious. Then what of worship? Is there no " new song " which, even in the intermediate regions of Paradise, our loved ones will sing? But, as the late Baron von Hügel said : " One never gets any spiritual ideas out of Spiritualism."

As for myself, I would far rather trust the picture contained in the " Dream of Gerontius," which proceeded from the mind of a poet and a saint, than any information which had filtered through the mind of a medium. The atmosphere of humility, contrition and worship which this poem suggests fully satisfies the longings of the human heart. Think of those magnificent words, if possible, as they are joined to Elgar's heavenly music—

> " Praise to the Holiest in the height,
>   And in the depth be praise;
> In all His words most wonderful,
>   Most sure in all His ways "—

and ask whether you would really wish to exchange this for the atmosphere of Feda, Moonshine and Redfeather and their trivialities.

CHAPTER V

CHRISTADELPHIANISM

THE Christadelphians, or Brothers of Christ, claim to be a repro-
duction of the primitive Church, and to have no founder but
Christ Himself. But in fact they take their rise from Dr. John
Thomas, a medical practitioner, who migrated from England to
America just one hundred years ago. There he was converted by
Walter Scott, founder of the American sect of the Campbellites,
and gave up medicine for theology. He studied the Scriptures
and gloried in his ignorance of other books and in not having
been " cursed with a theological education." He soon broke with
the Campbellites, asserting that they were as ignorant of the true
faith as was the rest of misguided Christendom. He preached
extensively in England and Scotland, Canada and the United
States, and invented the name Christadelphian to distinguish his
followers from Christians, who in his opinion were associated
with everything anti-Christian.

The Bible was his authority, and he admitted no errors in it.
Old and New Testaments were of equal value, as of course they
must always be to believers in verbal inspiration. It can be
imagined what astounding notions may result when a blank mind,
ignorant and contemptuous of history and of other literature,
turns to the English Bible with the conviction that the precise and
final truth is discoverable from any verse of it. The possible error
is only limited by the imaginative capacity of the inquirer. What
Dr. Thomas found may be briefly set out as follows :

Man was created for immortality, but became mortal by the fall
of Adam and Eve. He neither possesses, nor ever did possess, an
immortal spirit; his original immortality was a bodily one, to be
lived out on this material earth. But by faith in Jesus Christ, who

came to fulfil the promises made by God to the patriarchs, man may regain immortality. It will still be, however, a bodily immortality. The kingdom of Israel will be restored at Jerusalem in Palestine, which city must be rebuilt to serve as the headquarters of Christ when He returns to earth.

All this will strike the ordinary Christian with amazement. But it is put forward quite seriously, and it contains the whole principle of the Christadelphian creed. Dr. Thomas had a primitive mind, and he could not understand what the ordinary Christian means by " spiritual." It was for him a thing " shadowy, ghostly, unreal, nothingistic." Even God must have a personal form and must dwell in " some sanctified portion of the universe." The earth was the reality, and men with solid bodies living on it. This earth was to abide for ever. Angels are beings of ordinary personal shape and appearance. When fallen man dies " he returns again to his dust; he ceases to be, his thoughts perish; he is as though he had not been born." Here we have, as every intelligent Bible reader can see, the primitive notions of men before the faith in a resurrection and a spiritual existence arose. Those who follow John Thomas are living in the mental atmosphere of 500 B.C.

In spite of the fact that when man dies he utterly ceases to be, a resurrection and a judgment are expected when Christ returns to this earth in the flesh. This return was predicted by Thomas to take place in 1868, but he wisely allowed a possible period of forty-two years for the " subjugation of the nations." Accordingly, his biographer, Robert Roberts of Birmingham, writing shortly before 1910, claimed that the doctor's calculations could not be proved wrong until the year 1910 had passed. We need not make too much of the failure of this prediction, for thousands like it have been made by ignorant minds dwelling on the abstruse symbolism of Daniel and Revelation, and we know from experience that the non-fulfilment of a prediction never disconcerts those who believe in it. They count on the short memories of men, and simply push forward their date in order to keep their adherents in a state of suspense and hope.

It is not clear whether the judgment will take place immediately on Christ's return or after the complete establishment of His kingdom. But certainly the kingdom is not to be established peacefully. "The nations will have to resign their kingdoms to Him, a work unfortunately which they will not readily nor peacefully be disposed to perform." So there comes the war of Armageddon, in which the world kingdoms are overthrown. After that the world is peopled by mortals but ruled by the saints—that is, the Christadelphians—from Jerusalem. "Finally, however" (I am quoting from a recent booklet which tells us authoritatively what Christadelphians believe and teach), "this mortal element tires of the good and peace of the earth and the perfection of Divine government, and rebels against God their Creator and against Christ and the Saints, their King and Rulers." Then God "blots out entirely the mortal element and reveals the redeemed earth peopled with immortal saints."

The reader will notice how, at a time when Christians are trying to understand one another better, and when statesmen, through the Kellogg Pact and the League of Nations, are doing their best to usher in a period of peace and goodwill, these fanatics, like the British-Israelites, go about preaching a most horrible war which is soon to take place to enable God to fulfil His purposes with man. Can they never learn that "the wrath of man worketh not the righteousness of God"? Is our God, who showed His character in the Cross of Jesus, to be regarded as a bloodthirsty despot who "blots out," apparently without a pang, myriads of human beings, consigning them to extinction for ever in order that a few Christadelphians may reign in solitude on this earth? The notion would be ludicrous if it were not so diabolically blasphemous.

Yet these men, to whom war is an instrument of God's policy, a deliberately chosen weapon of His will, would not allow their adherents to serve in the last war. They made a great to-do because two Birmingham members became special constables. Munition making, however, was not forbidden. Since the present state of human society is in their idea hopelessly corrupt, they do not engage in any works of social or political betterment. They leave the world just as it is, until God comes to judge it. A more selfish, cowardly and anti-Christian spirit I find it hard to imagine.

It is not necessary to adduce theological errors, such as the denial of the Incarnation and of the doctrine of the Trinity, for these proceed from an inability to understand the real meaning of the Bible and of Christian theology. A great heresy may be judged by the conception it forms of God and by its attitude to men. The former I have already indicated sufficiently. As for the latter, a quotation from the booklet above referred to is illuminating: " The Christadelphians call upon all who wish to participate in these glories of the future to obey Christ's command through the Apostle John, to come out of the iniquitous system introduced originally by the Papacy, whose tenets have spread to England and are now to be discovered not only in the original form in the blasphemous ' Holy Roman Catholic Church,' but also in their [sic] offspring, the Anglican Church, and the minor forms of dissent."

So much for Christians! The rest of the world apparently is not worth considering.

For myself, I would prefer to take my chance with the Roman Catholics and the Baptists rather than to enjoy dominating the earth with the Christadelphians.

But what astounding arrogance is it for men thus to condemn wholesale their fellow-Christians, included among whom are the very men whose labours, and often whose deaths, have preserved for them the Scriptures from which they perversely draw their fantastic doctrines? This alone is enough to stamp their teaching as wrong.

CHAPTER VI

JUDGE RUTHERFORD

" MILLIONS now living will never die." From time to time we have seen this message on placards, and crowds have gone to hear the man who delivers it. Who are these hearers, and what is it that attracts them?

It is an unending puzzle. Doctrines that are absurd on the face of them; prophecies that have often proved false; descriptions of God's providence that shock the moral sense—all these come up again and again and appear to flourish. How can we explain it?

Until about half a century ago strong pressure was put upon men to adopt the beliefs favoured by whatever authority was in power. Parents compelled their children, society had its rigid standards, Church and State alike were at heart intolerant of departure from recognised beliefs. To-day we condemn this intolerance and laud freedom to the skies. We not only allow, we even encourage everybody to think as he likes. But we forget that the old method was not entirely unreasonable. It kept masses of simple people on sound lines, sternly forbidding them to indulge in extravagant notions not supported by the wisdom of the ages. This severe regimentation, though harmful to some, probably did more good than harm to the majority. The community contains many Peter Pans who never grow up, and these if left to themselves are far more likely to go wrong than right in difficult matters like religious belief.

We can never return to the old intolerant days, and ought never to want to; yet we must remember that many absurd beliefs of to-day are directly traceable to our go-as-you-please attitude, which throws a sort of sanctity over any man's opinion, however foolish it may be. And if a clever man wishes to trade on the credulity of the ignorant, he has now abundant freedom to do so, whereas in past days he would have been sternly repressed.

Human motives are often mixed, and the real forces that move men are difficult to discover. A self-interested man may have a strain of the genuine fanatic in him, while a fanatic may discover that his belief, be it as cranky as you like, brings him fame and fortune. And we cannot console ourselves with the thought that a belief which is patently proved to be false will disappear on that account. For each new generation, as it succeeds the one before it, does not inherit the experience of the old; it has to acquire its own. If I were to prophesy the end of the world in 1940 and it did not happen then, I should hide my face for shame and never wish to be seen again. But not so the religious quack. He knows that between 1930 and 1940 a new generation has been coming to maturity which, being unaware of what has happened in the past, will be eagerly interested in a new prophecy for 1950. To expose such a man is therefore of little use, for he will turn to the new generation and start afresh.

I have read much of Judge Rutherford's literature, and scanned a great deal more. His books have widely different titles, but they are filled with much the same material. The author attacks with great vehemence American politics and big business, contending that these are agencies of Satan and not of God. I know too little of America to contradict him on this point, but what he says would certainly not be true of England. There is plenty of wickedness among us, but it would be disloyal to God to despair of the world and to say, as Rutherford does, that God has given it into the control of Satan.

For the rest, we have the ordinary Christadelphian story of the approaching end of the world. The exact date is not given, but it is to happen " within a very short time." The battle of Armageddon is described in Biblical imagery all taken literally and without any knowledge of the times in which the book of Revelation was written and the purpose it then served. The saints are not to take part in the conflict; they are to be quiet and wait and

God will do everything for them. Lurid pictures are drawn of angels with swords about to slaughter bloated capitalists and crafty priests. The whole presentation is repulsive. The eternal kingdom is to be established on this earth. Questions that arise in our minds, such as whether people will grow old, or marry, or others be born, in this everlasting earth-life, are ignored; doubtless they do not occur to the people for whom this literature is designed. The coming Golden Age is illustrated by pictures resembling a Garden City or the advertisement of a Building Society.

A rudimentary theology is outlined, capable of appealing to the immature and illiterate. God is called " Jehovah God," as if He had a name. Jesus Christ is His Son, not in the Christian sense of being the " Word of God," the " very image " of the Father's substance (Heb. i. 3)—this relationship of essence is expressly denied—but in a crude Arian sense, a sort of semi-divine personality hovering between earth and heaven. The doctrine of the Trinity is rejected. Rutherford quarrels with the Modernists because (according to his notions) they do not believe the Bible; and also with the Fundamentalists because, although they believe in the Bible, their belief differs from his own. Such is the result of allowing men freedom of thought before they know how to think; each must not only be right, but solely and absolutely right, all others being hopelessly wrong.

The American Press, after being viciously assailed by Rutherford, has turned upon him to ask inconsiderate questions about the finances of his movement. Such curiosity is not unreasonable, for, to quote from one of the Judge's own works, " In a year of world depression, 1932, Judge Rutherford's books and booklets announcing Jehovah's kingdom were distributed to the extent of 22,213,639 copies." The word " distributed " is a euphemism for " sold." Rutherford says that they are sold at a little over cost price and that the negligible profits go to the International Bible Students' Association. But of the books that I have seen there are a dozen or more costing 2s. or thereabouts apiece in England. Though gaudily coloured, they are of the cheapest possible make and must be produced (when we consider that the first printing of each is a million copies and one had reached over five millions in 1928) for very little. If only an average of a penny a copy profit be allowed, the 22 million odd would have brought in well over £90,000 for 1932—a tidy income for somebody. But this is a ludicrously small figure; an average of 6d. a copy would be nearer the mark. If Rutherford's figures are correct, and he has sold " upwards of 130 million pieces of literature " since he began ten years ago, the bosses of American business might well envy him. We cannot wonder that men call attention to this aspect of Rutherford's campaign, especially as no other writer's name appears anywhere and the International Bible Students' Association, for all we know, may be merely Rutherford himself.

It is difficult to persuade people that the Church, with its faith that has stood the test of centuries, is still worth listening to. Many will run after any new sensation and believe the most incredible things. All we can do is to warn the young and inexperienced that these strange paths lead invariably to spiritual disaster. In the Church men can have fellowship (and how gladly it is offered to-day!), grace through prayer and sacrament, and opportunity to learn humbly of the things of God. The Church has many faults and needs constant penitence and renewal. But as I read one after another the accounts of these pitiable attempts to supersede her, I cannot help turning back to her in fresh gratitude and love. She gives room for the soul to live in and to grow. And so long as I have the power I will warn others of the peril of deserting her, " whether," as Ezekiel wrote, " they will hear, or whether they will forbear."

CHAPTER VII

THEOSOPHY

THE Christian religion arose in a land which lies midway between East and West. We see a Divine Providence in this, for no religion which did not partake of the characteristics of both East and West could hope to appeal to the whole human race. In its growth, however, the Church went westward far more than eastward, and as a result the practical side of religion, congenial to the Western mind, overshadowed the mystical and imaginative side which is characteristic of the East. In the latter half of the nineteenth century there was a re-discovery of the ancient religious thought of India, and many people in England and America, brought up in a rather cold and bare scientific and theological atmosphere, were fascinated by it. For Theosophy, or the "wisdom of the divine," is a re-hash of Oriental, chiefly Indian, thought, and, false and foolish as it certainly is, it does nevertheless set the mind working and open out a universe larger and richer than the one present to the mind of many Christians.

Theosophy, like Christian Science, owes its origin to a woman. Helena Petrovna Blavatsky (the surname comes from the man she married in 1848 and left three months after the marriage) was born in 1831 in Russia, but of German descent. After what she herself called a "stormy life," in which she had "run amuck against society and the established proprieties," she settled in America in 1873. She possessed in marked degree the powers of a medium, and was attracted by all that was occult, magical and weird. In America she practised Spiritualism, in conjunction with Colonel Olcott, and her control was called John King. She seems to have believed in him, for she wrote that " John King is a definite, living, spiritual personality. Whether devil or good spirit, he is at all events a spirit and not the medium's prototype."

But she met the fate of most mediums, being detected in gross fraud. Thus discredited, she had to seek another line of action, and she turned to the Eastern religions. By reading a large number of out-of-the-way books on magic and demonology she composed a work entitled *Isis Unveiled,* which claimed to be a revelation of the essential truth lying behind all religions, sent from the Great White Brotherhood, a company of adepts in the divine wisdom, who dwelt in Tibet, a land which unfortunately is at present too inaccessible to allow of any investigation of their existence. The work was, in fact, almost wholly composed of passages taken out of books which she had read. With this scripture the Theosophical Society was founded by Olcott and herself, who were called the " Theosophical Twins."

Mrs. Besant, the recent head of the Theosophical Society, thus describes the spiritualistic exposure to which I have alluded, and which is amply proved by unimpeachable evidence : " She (*i.e.,* Madame Blavatsky) endeavoured first to collaborate with the American Spiritualists, but, failing in this, she, with Olcott, founded the Theosophical Society." Let the ordinary Christian take note, and remember the kind of people he will be dealing with when he approaches Theosophy.

America having proved an unsuitable home, Madame Blavatsky and Olcott sailed for Bombay. John King, the spirit control, now vanishes, and is replaced by two members of the Great White Brotherhood, who had selected her above all human beings to be the recipient of the divine wisdom. Their names are Mahatma Morya and Koot Hoomi. They were in mystic communication with her. A sacred shrine, with a portrait of Koot Hoomi in it, before which Hindus bowed reverently and offered incense, was set in the wall of a room which adjoined Madame Blavatsky's bedroom. Letters placed in this shrine were miraculously removed and answers from Koot Hoomi found there a few days after.

Broken saucers were mended. These miracles were a source of much delight to Hindus, who found their ancient religions being vindicated against Christianity by these immortal teachers who dwelt in Tibet and were even now revealing their wisdom through Madame Blavatsky.

But alas! the Psychical Research Society sent out an investigator, who soon discovered the fraud. A sliding panel at the back of the shrine gave access to Madame Blavatsky's chamber, and most of the letters were in her handwriting and style, even to characteristic mis-spellings. Only a very few of her associates knew of the existence of this panel. But the revelation made it necessary for her to leave India.

After Madame Blavatsky, Mrs. Besant became the chief figure in the Theosophical world, aided by Mr. Leadbeater, who was formerly a minister of the Church of England. Suffice it to say that both these hold that Madame Blavatsky was an apprentice of the Great White Brotherhood—that is, a human being who had resolved to devote herself utterly to the service of mankind and to communicate to them the hidden wisdom of the ages. Not a word of the scandals and frauds, more numerous than I have had space to mention, is admitted. Of Mrs. Besant's writings in defence of Madame Blavatsky, Dr. J. N. Farquhar, who has made an exhaustive study of the subject, says: " These books and pamphlets are by far the most unreliable literature that it has ever been my sad fate to have to study."

It may be asked: " Are we to condemn a teaching because it has a sordid history? Must we not judge a tree by its fruits and not by its roots?" If so large and essential a part of the history offends the moral sense, as is certainly the case with Theosophy, I think the teaching is vitiated thereby. But there must be something in Theosophy which causes it to appeal to so many. What exactly is this?

Mrs. Besant maintains that Theosophy has three aims: (1) to promote the brotherhood of man; (2) to further the study of comparative religion, science and philosophy; and (3) to investigate the unexplained laws of Nature and the powers latent in man.

The first is a teaching of Christianity, though we must admit that Christians have not always regarded it as a very vital article of their faith. The second is wholly admirable. But we are bound to say that Theosophy has contributed nothing of value to the study of comparative religion. No Theosophist would be recognised as a fellow-worker among Orientalists. And as for science, Theosophy presents us with something very different from the science we know, a knowledge patiently won by observation and experiment. Theosophic science is a farrago of assertions about the nature of the universe, depending upon the alleged intuitions of Mrs. Besant or Mr. Leadbeater, and to be accepted without question on their *ipse dixit*.

It is under the third heading, in its teaching about the abnormal activities of the human mind, clairvoyance, telepathy, hypnotism and the like, that Theosophy proves attractive to many. It promises occult knowledge, leading to power, to those who accept its discipline. But the cost is great. A promise of absolute secrecy and instant obedience has to be made. The votaries, by long meditation in one direction, gradually have their minds moulded by the *guru* under whom they place themselves. They read little else but Theosophic literature, and become at last, as they are meant to become, incapable of independent thought or criticism. Minds so receptive can be filled with any wild fancies that come along, and who is to decide between these, false and misleading as they often must be, and the occasional genuine intuitive visions of the spiritual world?

According to Theosophy, the world exists not only as the physical entity which we discern, but in six other planes which interpenetrate the physical, all of which the practised master can detect by clairvoyance. To these planes names are given—Emotional or Astral, Mental, Intuitional, Spiritual, Monadic and Divine. At death the soul passes to the first, where it stays till its passions are spent; then to the second, where its " thought-forces," whatever these may be, are likewise spent. After some period of dwelling on the higher planes the soul is re-incarnated on earth, and this happens over and over again.

Now undoubtedly there are more things in heaven and earth than are dreamed of in our philosophy, and Christians, as I have before admitted, often hold a bare and narrow conception of the universe. A more vivid notion of the richness and depth and mystery of things would be beneficial to most of us; and to reach this the practice of meditation, and the use of the imagination, should form a considerable part of our thought and prayer life. But if we are to be preserved from error there are three cautions to be observed.

First, we must check our fancies by scientific knowledge, wherever this is available. Science does not penetrate to the depths of being; as yet it operates, probably, on the surface; but it is accurate so far as it goes, and it has brought untold blessings to men, enabling us to heal and prevent disease, to assuage pain, to travel widely and to communicate with loved ones far away. It would be the height of folly to trust in " intuitions " which cannot be verified rather than in patient research, more especially since these intuitions are extravagant beyond words, filling men's heads, as Dr. Farquhar justly remarks, with froth instead of knowledge.

Secondly, we must demand the Christian moral standard. We are told that these clairvoyant powers, by which the so-called knowledge is obtained, have nothing to do with purity of character. They can exist, and have existed, as Theosophic history shows, in men and women who lie and cheat and are guilty of every immorality. The human heart revolts against the claim that God will speak through such as these.

Lastly, our meditation must have as its object no other than God, the Blessed Trinity, Father, Son and Holy Spirit. Theosophy has no real God, such as the loving Father revealed by Jesus Christ, but only an unknowable, impersonal Being. And Jesus, the Word of God, takes a place beside the mythical White

Brotherhood who reveal their secrets to Mrs. Besant and Mr. Leadbeater.

If anyone doubts the fairness of these observations, let him read J. N. Farquhar's *Modern Religious Movements in India,* pp. 208-291, with the authorities quoted there. His conclusion is that Theosophy is a " poisonous anti-Christian system."

CHAPTER VIII

ROSICRUCIANISM

I

"Omne ignotum pro magnifico," said Tacitus (Keep a thing secret, and men will exaggerate its importance). So the fascination of secret societies is world-wide and never-ending. But the time is long past when teachers of new truth had to remain hidden for fear of their lives. To-day no message deserves a hearing unless it will come out into the open and declare itself plainly.

At the beginning of the seventeenth century, in Germany, a number of curious pamphlets were issued which professed to come from the Brotherhood of the Rosy Cross—whence the name Rosicrucian. Its sign was a rose fixed upon a cross. The founder was reputed to be one Christian Rosenkreuz, who had died one hundred and twenty years before, but had ordered his few followers to keep strict silence about his plans for that length of time. Now, however, the pamphlets declared, the silence was to be broken. A universal Reformation was about to be accomplished, greater than the Protestant Reformation which had only recently occurred. Men were invited to join the Brotherhood and help forward the Reformation. A description was given of Rosenkreuz, how he had travelled in the East and acquired stores of secret wisdom. A fantastic tale, entitled " The Chymical Marriage," told of the adventures of Rosenkreuz through fairy-tale scenes until at last he is made a " Knight of the Golden Stone "—*i.e.*, one initiated into the mysteries of alchemy and magic. All these writings may be read in A. E. Waite's *The Real History of the Rosicrucians*. Not one of them shows the least trace of any inspiration or of any wisdom beyond what was well known to the world of that time. " The Chymical Marriage," with its almost unending succession of gilded chambers, gorgeous feasts, mystic inscriptions and uncanny ceremonies, is a thoroughly wearisome work except for those who delight in the absurdest of day-dreams.

The general ideas underlying the supposed Brotherhood, when all extravagance is stripped away, were simple enough. The Rosicrucians were to be travelling physicians, giving their services without fee or reward. They professed to have secret remedies for diseases, and to be able to raise the dead, transport themselves rapidly through space, and perform the *magnum opus*—*i.e.*, turn base metals into gold. Some, it is true, have denied this, saying that the Rosicrucians meant their claim to be spiritually understood, the true *magnum opus* being knowledge of God or of Nature. This may be correct, but it is certain that later Rosicrucians were alchemists and magicians.

Many inquiries were made through published letters and pamphlets (for the Rosicrucian writings bore no address) by persons wishing to join the Brotherhood. But none was ever answered. The affair may have been a hoax. There is, indeed, no evidence that Rosenkreuz or his Brotherhood ever existed. If they did, it is hard to see why they should have arranged to publish an invitation and then ignore those who responded to it. The symbol of the rose and cross originated long before their time. Others have used it, and Freemasons still do. What meaning the Rosicrucians meant it to convey has never been explained.

We must remember that these events happened before the days when science had opened a door to the secrets of nature. We know now that by well-tried methods, intelligible and above board, knowledge of the universe may be obtained. Any man may discover this knowledge if he has the necessary patience and humility. Human observation and reason are the sole means. No educated man to-day would believe for a moment in the reality of occult powers apart from verifiable evidence of their working, which has never been given. But in the past men dreamed that there were magical processes which, if only you could light upon them, would give you immediate command over nature. Some of these men were working towards a scientific method; others were mere quacks and impostors. But both had a large share of the credulity of their age. We can no more accept the stories of the wonders they were said to have wrought than we could take the Arabian Nights as serious history.

The Rosicrucians, after the sensation of their first appearance in Germany, disappear from the foreground of history, but crop up from time to time in certain writers who, while generally professing not to belong to their Society, yet practise their methods and praise their alleged knowledge. One Michael Maier introduced the Society to Robert Fludd in England. Fludd lived in Elizabeth's reign and wrote many weird books of mystical speculation on the constitution of the universe. The origin of these speculations is well known to students; they are derived from the Neo-Platonists and the successors of a mystical writer calling himself Dionysius the Areopagite—*i.e.*, claiming to be the Dionysius whom St. Paul met at Athens, but really belonging to the fifth century—together with the Kabbalists, or Jewish mystical speculators. It would be highly improper to treat all these flights of the imagination with contempt, for they were based upon a conviction that God was in the world and that His workings could be seen and known. Yet they were mingled with so much that was crude and puerile, even for those days, that their value is exceedingly small. Every object and event in nature—stars, clouds, storms and all else—was attributed to the action of some elemental spirit, and rational causes were derided. Such an outlook, if it had prevailed universally, would have been fatal to the growth of science, which has had so powerful and beneficent an influence upon life.

There has been a Rosicrucian Society in England since 1886. It claims historical connexion with the original German Society, but advances no evidence in support of the claim. From this, apparently, have sprung affiliated societies in different parts of the world. Hastings' *Encyclopædia of Religion and Ethics* contains an article on the Rosicrucians by Arthur Cadbury Jones. It tells us nothing but what can be obtained from well-known writings, omitting the absurdities. When we feel we are on the point of being enlightened the writer takes refuge in vague generalities and hints about a hidden wisdom which cannot be communicated to ordinary men. I was interested to learn that Bishop Pearson, author of the famous *Exposition of the Creed*, was a Rosicrucian and formed a lodge of the Society in London. The evidence given is " ' Occult Science,' which forms vol. xxxi. of the *Encyclopædia Metropolitana* of 1845." On looking up this reference I could find no vol. xxxi. and no treatment throughout the Encyclopædia of " Occult Science " or any subject like it. Perhaps these evidences are not visible to profane eyes! The nearest approach to information given by Mr. Cadbury Jones is as follows, that the members of the Society carry on " investigations into the uses of vegetable drugs and the relief of disease by means of coloured lights and by hypnotic processes; there are numerous physicians using these means, which are freely supplied, but these doctors are not necessarily pledged members of the fraternity." Unless we are told what the " lights " and " hypnotic processes " are (and there can be no reason for secrecy about things beneficial to man) and who are the physicians who use them, the statement is about as valuable as if I were to say that I had communicated the doctrine of relativity to Dr. Einstein, but had asked him to keep dark about it.

It seemed necessary to begin with this historical sketch. Yet I have no doubt that what readers will most desire to hear about is the modern development which hails from California, with which I shall now deal.

II

Amid the welter of superstition which afflicts the world to-day something which purports to be a popularisation of the Rosicrucian teachings has arisen in America. I have before me a book entitled *The Rosicrucian Cosmo-Conception*, or *Mystic Christianity*, described in the sub-title as *An Elementary Treatise upon Man's Past Evolution, Present Constitution and Future Development*, by Max Heindel. This is issued from the International Headquarters of the Rosicrucian Fellowship at Mount Ecclesia, Oceanside, California. The writer keeps carefully to the old phraseology; he is not a brother of the Order, but only a disciple. He is publishing the elements of Rosicrucian teaching, "because the world's intelligence is growing to the necessary point of comprehension." I pass on the compliment to my readers. But with true American shrewdness he insists on possessing a monopoly of truth. "This work is one of the first few fragments of the Rosicrucian knowledge being publicly given out. All that has been printed as such, previous to the last few years, is the work of either charlatans or traitors." Thus are Germany and Great Britain quietly wiped off the map.

The reason why California is now the Headquarters of the Fellowship is as follows. "Southern California offers exceptional opportunities for spiritual growth, because of the ether atmosphere being denser than in any other part of the world, and Mount Ecclesia, as the Rosicrucian Fellowship Headquarters are called, is particularly favoured in this respect." (The quotation is given exactly.) No doubt this explains the "uplift" we get from Californian films.

Now let us at once admit that no one could write a book of over 600 reasonably coherent pages without saying some things that are wise and true. The writer exhibits much of that amiable aspiration and sympathy characteristic of American humanistic teaching. An introductory poem, "Creed or Christ," is couched in the ordinary "What's the use of Creeds? Why can't we all love one another?" style. It gives the impression that these people slither over the surface of life and never meet its sharp edges. That impression is deepened by the thoroughly Oriental treatment of the problem of evil. Souls are reborn again and again to the kind of existence they deserve. The explanation of natural catastrophes is so ingenious that I give it in the writer's own words, if the reader can keep his blood cool while he scans it. " It is generally profligate and degenerate peoples who succumb to these catastrophes. They, together with others whose destiny, self-generated under the law of Consequence, for various reasons, involves a violent death, are gathered from many lands, by the superhuman forces, to the point where the eruption is to occur. To the thoughtful the volcanic outbursts of Vesuvius, for instance, will afford corroboration of this statement." This is a libel on the human race. There were thousands of people in Herculaneum and Pompeii, in Lisbon and Messina, as good, loving and brave as the inhabitants of ethereal California (which, by the way, has also had an earthquake lately). Not so are the ways of God to be justified to men. Besides, for Christians this harsh theory is directly contradicted by our Lord in His reply to the question about the Galilean victims of Pilate and the Tower of Siloam (St. Luke xiii.).

Whether the system outlined in this book has any connexion with the original Rosicrucians (if such existed) or no, I cannot say, for no evidence is given us on which to judge. But the system itself, and its real origin, is clear enough. It is a mingling of Theosophy, Re-incarnation theories, and Occultism generally, with a confused misunderstanding of the teachings of science. It is one sign of the desperate struggle which the East is making to-day to gain ascendency over the minds of the lesser educated sections of Western society. As such it is more dangerous than many plain men, reading the harmless-looking pages of this book, might imagine. Christ is indeed universal, the Lord of all men. But it is the West which has accepted Him, imperfectly enough, if you like, but still really. He dominates us. And the East, recognising His superiority, tries, not to accept, but to utilise Him. All books of the theosophic type pay lip-service to Christ, as this one does; but when you examine them you find that under fair-sounding phrases they hide something clean contrary both to Jesus Christ and to the Christianity which has sprung from Him.

The widest variations of our religion have far more kinship with each other than with this Oriental superstition.

A similar process occurred in the second century. Fantastic thinkers of the Oriental type, observing the rise of the Christian Church, tried to graft their theories upon it. The system of thought thus brought into being was called Gnosticism. In place of the One Father and the Eternal Word and Holy Spirit, Gnosticism substituted an original Unknowable, with a long succession of Beings descending from Him. Christ was one of these. The system described in the book before us, with numerous worlds and countless semi-divine Existences, is just a new variety of Gnosticism. God—that is, the Creator of our Solar System— is a long way down in the scale of Divine Being. "When the name 'God' is used," says the author, "it is always uncertain whether The Absolute, The One Existence, is meant; or The Supreme Being, who is the Great Architect of the Universe; or God, who is the Architect of our Solar System." So the Holy Spirit is the "Race God," and is the same as Jehovah, who is also the "Regent of the Moon," whatever that may mean.

Gnosticism means "a system of Knowledge," as opposed to faith. The Gnostic teachers claimed to know, by virtue of an esoteric tradition derived from Jesus, but not openly proclaimed in the Gospels or the doctrine of the Church, the truth of their complicated theories. So Mr. Max Heindel has access to a hidden source of knowledge. After the Transfiguration Jesus commanded His disciples to "tell no man." "This," comments our author, "was to be, for thousands of years, an esoteric teaching." All the narrative tells us is that our Lord forbade His disciples to proclaim abroad the vision, the sign of His Messiahship, until He had risen from the dead. Then they both proclaimed it and described it in three Gospels. It is sheer nonsense to talk of esoteric traditions in this connexion, or indeed in any other that has to do with Christian origins. For never was any religion proclaimed to the world in a manner more clear, aboveboard and rational than was early Christianity.

Another point of contact both with Gnosticism and with Theosophy is the absolute authority of the teacher. "Unwavering confidence in the teacher is absolutely necessary." I agree that if anyone is to believe all the extraordinary assertions of this book he can only do so on the bare *ipse dixit* of a teacher; for neither reason nor ordinary experience will bear them out. How does the teacher know? He is a clairvoyant and can see all kinds of things that are hidden from us. "The occultist sees the Ego and can trace its path after it has passed out of the body at death until it has reappeared on earth in a new birth. Therefore to him no 'belief' is necessary." The chances of deception here, self-deception and the deception of others, seem very great indeed. Faith in the Christian sense means loving attachment of ourselves to a Person whom we wish to serve and whose voice we hear speaking through His Spirit and through the Church which He has preserved and guided for nineteen hundred years. There is nothing irrational about this, and such a faith brings its own verification as the years pass. But to take a master who says that he can see these amazing things, world above world, spiritual beings inhabiting every star and planet, souls of the departed in their journeyings and rebirths, and to believe all he tells us without criticism, with the faint hope that one day, after living many forgotten lives on this earth, we may develop to the spiritual heights which he has reached and be able to see what he sees, this is an extravagance of credulity altogether foreign to our religion.

Many may think it not worth while to spend time refuting beliefs which are so palpably absurd. But these theosophic circles beguile the unwary. Speculations about astral bodies and ethereal worlds may be innocent enough, but they lead to Astrology and other practices which educated men have long ago abandoned. And whatever the author may say about the "Rosicrucian Interpretation of Christianity," this is in truth a perversion and not an interpretation. Much is made of the fact that initiation into the Fellowship is without cost; no Rosicrucian teacher must ask

for fees. But at the end of this work there are no less than six-
teen pages of advertisements of books and pamphlets, most of
them costing 2 or 3 dollars, together with a " Correspondence
Course." There is enough here to reward the author for the
trouble he has taken to spread the Rosicrucian teaching.

PRINTED IN GREAT BRITAIN BY
BILLING AND SONS LTD., GUILDFORD AND ESHER